HOW TO ENJOY YOUR LIFE AND YOUR JOB

HOW TO ENJOY YOUR LIFE AND YOUR JOB

Selections from
*How to Win Friends and Influence People
and How to Stop Worrying and Start Living*

DALE CARNEGIE

foreword by
DOROTHY CARNEGIE

Vermilion
LONDON

10

Published in 1998 by Vermilion, an imprint of Ebury Publishing.

First Published in the United States of America by Simon and Schuster in 1948.

First published in Great Britain by Cedar Books in 1989.

Ebury Publishing is a division of the Random House Group.

The Random House Group Limited Reg. No. 954009

Addresses for companies within the Random House Group can be found at www.randomhouse.co.uk

A CIP catalogue record for this book is available from the British Library.

Printed and bound by CPI Group (UK) Ltd, Croydon, CR0 4YY

ISBN 9780749305932

The Random House Group Limited supports The Forest Stewardship Council (FSC®), the leading international forest certification organisation. Our books carrying the FSC label are printed on FSC® certified paper. FSC is the only forest certifi... ...scheme endorsed by the leading environmental ...anisations, incl... ...found at

Contents

EXCERPTS FROM
How to Stop Worrying and Start Living

PART ONE

Seven Ways to Peace and Happiness

EXCERPTS FROM
How to Win Friends and Influence People

PART TWO

Fundamental Techniques in Handling People

PART THREE

Ways to Win People to Your Way of Thinking

PART FOUR

Ways to Change People Without Giving Offense or Arousing Resentment

Foreword

Did you ever stop to think that most of us spend the greater part of our lives on the job—whatever that job may be?

This means that our attitude toward our job can determine whether our days are filled with excitement and the sense of fulfillment that comes from top performance—or with frustration, boredom, and fatigue.

Dale Carnegie Training® is designed to help you get the most out of your working day in terms of job-satisfaction by getting the most out of yourself *all* the time. As you study these pages, evaluate your own approach to life and people. Then start to build on your strengths and discover how many talents and abilities you actually have that you didn't even know you had—and how much fun it is to use these abilities.

This book is a collection of chapters selected from the revised editions of Dale Carnegie's two best sellers, *How to Win Friends and Influence People* and *How to Stop Worrying and Start Living*. We have selected those portions of each book most relevant to people like yourself. You want more fulfillment in your life, a sense of harmony and purpose, a feeling that you're making the best use of your inner resources—and this book will help you achieve these aims.

Participation in Dale Carnegie Training® is an adventure in self-discovery; and it could be a turning point in your life. You already possess hidden assets within yourself that can make your life glorious. All you need now is the determination to uncover and use them.

Dorothy Carnegie

Chairman of the Board
Dale Carnegie & Associates, Inc.

PART ONE

SEVEN WAYS
TO PEACE
AND
HAPPINESS

Dale Carnegie wrote his book *How to Stop Worrying and Start Living* to show that life is very much what we make it. If we first learn to accept ourselves, seeing the good as clearly as the not-so-good, and then get busy doing the things necessary to reach our goals, we will be less likely to have either the need or the inclination to lose time and energy worrying.

1

Find Yourself and Be Yourself: Remember, There Is No One Else on Earth Like You

I have a letter from Mrs. Edith Allred, of Mount Airy, North Carolina: "As a child, I was extremely sensitive and shy," she says in her letter. "I was always overweight and my cheeks made me look even fatter than I was. I had an old-fashioned mother who thought it was foolish to make clothes look pretty. She always said: 'Wide will wear while narrow will tear'; and she dressed me accordingly. I never went to parties; never had any fun; and when I went to school, I never joined the other children in outside activities, not even athletics. I was morbidly shy. I felt I was 'different' from everybody else and entirely undesirable.

"When I grew up, I married a man who was several years my senior. But I didn't change. My in-laws were a poised and self-confident family. They were everything I should have been but simply was not. I tried my best to be like them, but I couldn't. Every attempt they made to draw me out of myself only drove me further into my shell. I became nervous and irritable. I avoided all friends. I got so bad I even dreaded the sound of the doorbell ringing! I was a failure. I knew it; and I was afraid my husband would find it out. So, whenever we were in public, I tried to be gay, and overacted my part. I knew I overacted; and I would be miserable for days afterwards. At last I became so unhappy that I could see no point in prolonging my existence. I began to think of suicide."

What happened to change this unhappy woman's life? Just a chance remark!

"A chance remark," Mrs. Allred continued, "transformed my whole life. My mother-in-law was talking one day of how she brought her children up, and she said, 'No matter what happened, I always insisted on their being themselves.' . . . 'On being themselves.' . . . That remark is what did it! In a flash, I realized I had brought all this misery on myself by trying to fit myself into a pattern to which I did not conform.

"I changed overnight! I started being myself. I tried to make a study of my own personality. Tried to find out *what I was*. I studied my strong points. I learned all I could about colors and styles, and dressed in a way that I felt was becoming to me. I reached out to make friends. I joined an organization—a small one at first—and was petrified with fright when they put me on a program. But each time I spoke, I gained a little courage. It took a long while—but today I have more happiness than I ever dreamed possible. In rearing my own children, I have always taught them the lesson I had to learn from such bitter experience: *No matter what happens, always be yourself!*"

This problem of being unwilling to be yourself is "as old as history," says Dr. James Gordon Gilkey, "and as universal as human life." This problem of being unwilling to be yourself is the hidden spring behind many neuroses and psychoses and complexes. Angelo Patri has written thirteen books and thousands of syndicated newspaper articles on the subject of child training, and he says: "Nobody is so miserable as he who longs to be somebody and something other than the person he is in body and mind."

This craving to be something you are not is especially rampant in Hollywood. Sam Wood, one of Hollywood's best-known directors, said the greatest headache he has with aspiring young actors is exactly this problem: to make them be themselves. They all want to be second-rate Lana Turners or third-rate Clark Gables. "The public has already had that flavor," Sam Wood keeps telling them; "now it wants something else."

Before he started directing such pictures as *Goodbye, Mr. Chips* and *For Whom the Bell Tolls,* Sam Wood spent years in the real-estate business, developing sales personalities. He declares that the same principles apply in the business world as in the world of moving pictures. You won't get anywhere playing the ape. You can't be a parrot. "Experience has taught me," says Sam Wood, "that it is safest to drop, as quickly as possible, people who pretend to be what they aren't."

I asked Paul Boynton, then employment director for a major oil company, what is the biggest mistake people make in applying for jobs. He ought to know: he has interviewed more than sixty thousand job seekers; and he has written a book entitled *6 Ways to Get a Job.* He replied: "The biggest mistake people make in applying for jobs is in not being themselves. Instead of taking their hair down and being completely frank, they often try to give you the answers they think you want." But it doesn't work, because nobody wants a phony. Nobody ever wants a counterfeit coin.

A certain daughter of a streetcar conductor had to learn that lesson the hard way. She longed to be a singer. But her face was her misfortune. She had a large mouth and protruding buck teeth. When she first sang in public—in a New Jersey night club—she tried to pull down her upper lip to cover her teeth. She tried to act "glamorous." The results? She made herself ridiculous. She was headed for failure.

However, there was a man in this night club who heard the girl sing and thought she had talent. "See here," he said bluntly, "I've been watching your performance and I know what it is you're trying to hide. You're ashamed of your teeth!" The girl was embarrassed, but the man continued, "What of it? Is there any particular crime in having buck teeth? Don't try to hide them! Open your mouth, and the audience will love you when they see you're not ashamed. Besides," he said shrewdly, "those teeth you're trying to hide may make your fortune!"

Cass Daley took his advice and forgot about her teeth. *From that time on,* she thought only about her audience. She opened her mouth wide and sang with such gusto and enjoyment that she became a top star in movies and radio. Other comedians tried to copy *her!*

The renowned William James was speaking of people who had never found themselves when he declared that the average person develops only ten percent of his or her latent mental abilities. "Compared to what we ought to be," he wrote, "we are only half awake. We are making use of only a small part of our physical and mental resources. Stating the thing broadly, human individuals thus far live within their limits. They possess powers of various sorts which they habitually fail to use."

You and I have such abilities, so let's not waste a second worrying because we are not like other people. You are something new in this world. Never before, since the beginning of time, has there ever been anybody exactly like you; and never again throughout all the ages to come will there ever be anybody exactly like you again. The science of genetics informs us that you are what you are largely as a result of twenty-four chromosomes contributed by your father and twenty-four chromosomes contributed by your mother. These forty-eight chromosomes comprise everything that determines what you inherit. In each chromosome there may be, says Amram Scheinfeld, "anywhere from scores to hundreds of genes—with a single gene, in some cases, able to change the whole life of an individual." Truly, we are "fearfully and wonderfully" made.

Even after your mother and father met and mated, there was only one chance in 300,000 billion that the person who is specifically you would be born! In other words, if you had 300,000 billion brothers and sisters, they might all have been different from you. Is all this guesswork? No. It is a scientific fact. If you would like to read more about it, consult *You and Heredity*, by Amram Scheinfeld.

I can talk with conviction about this subject of being yourself because I feel deeply about it. I know what I am talking about. I know from bitter and costly experience. To illustrate: when I first came to New York from the cornfields of Missouri, I enrolled in the American Academy of Dramatic Arts. I aspired to be an actor. I had what I thought was a brilliant idea, a shortcut to success, an idea so simple, so foolproof, that I couldn't understand why thousands of ambitious people hadn't already discovered it. It was this: I would study how the famous actors of that day—John Drew, Walter Hampden, and Otis Skinner—got their effects. Then I would imitate the best points of each one of them and make myself into a shining, triumphant combination of all of them. How silly! How absurd! I had to waste years of my life imitating other people before it penetrated through my thick Missouri skull that I had to be myself, and that I couldn't possibly be anyone else.

That distressing experience ought to have taught me a lasting lesson. But it didn't. Not me. I was too dumb. I had to learn it all over again. Several years later, I set out to write what I hoped would be the best book on public speaking for businessmen that had ever been written. I had the same foolish idea about writing this book that I had formerly had about acting: I was going to *borrow* the ideas of a lot of other writers and put them all in one book—a book that would have everything. So I got scores of books on public speaking and spent a year incorporating their ideas into my manuscript. But it finally dawned on me once again that I was playing the fool. This hodgepodge of other men's ideas that I had written was so synthetic, so dull, that no businessman would ever plod through it. So I tossed a year's work into the wastebasket and started all over again. This time I said to myself: "You've got to be Dale Carnegie, with all his faults and limitations. You can't possibly be anybody else." So I quit trying to be a combination of other men, and rolled up my sleeves and did what I should have done in the first place: I wrote a textbook on public speaking out of my own experiences, observations, and convictions as a speaker and a teacher of speaking. I learned—for all time, I hope—the lesson that Sir Walter Raleigh learned. (I am *not* talking about the Sir Walter who threw his coat in the mud for the queen to step on. I am talking about the Sir Walter Raleigh who was professor of English literature at Oxford back in 1904.) "I can't write a book commensurate with Shakespeare," he said, "but I can write a book by me."

Be yourself. Act on the sage advice that Irving Berlin gave the late George Gershwin. When Berlin and Gershwin first met, Berlin was famous but Gershwin was a struggling young composer working for thirty-five dollars a week in Tin Pan Alley. Berlin, impressed by Gershwin's ability, offered Gershwin a job as his musical secretary at almost three times the salary he was then getting. "But don't take the job," Berlin advised. "If you do, you may develop into a second-rate Berlin. But if you insist on being yourself, someday you'll become a first-rate Gershwin."

Gershwin heeded that warning and slowly transformed

himself into one of the significant American composers of his generation.

Charle Chaplin, Will Rogers, Mary Margaret McBride, Gene Autry, and millions of others had to learn the lesson I am trying to hammer home in this chapter. They had to learn the hard way—just as I did.

When Charlie Chaplin first started making films, the director of the picture insisted on Chaplin's imitating a popular German comedian of that day. Charlie Chaplin got nowhere until he acted himself. Bob Hope had a similar experience: spent years in a singing-and-dancing act—and got nowhere until he began to wisecrack and be himself. Will Rogers twirled a rope in vaudeville for years without saying a word. He got nowhere until he discovered his unique gift for humor and began to talk as he twirled his rope.

When Mary Margaret McBride first went on the air, she tried to be an Irish comedian and failed. When she tried to be just what she was—a plain country girl from Missouri— she became one of the most popular radio stars in New York.

When Gene Autry tried to get rid of his Texas accent and dressed like city boys and claimed he was from New York, people merely laughed behind his back. But when he started twanging his banjo and singing cowboy ballads, Gene Autry started out on a career that made him the world's most popular cowboy both in pictures and on the radio.

You are something new in this world. Be glad of it. Make the most of what nature gave you. In the last analysis, all art is autobiographical. You can sing only what you are. You can paint only what you are. You must be what your experiences, your environment, and your heredity have made you. For better or for worse, you must cultivate your own little garden. For better or for worse, you must play your own little instrument in the orchestra of life.

As Emerson said in his essay on "Self-Reliance":

"There is a time in every man's education when he arrives at the conviction that envy is ignorance; that imitation is suicide; that he must take himself for better, for worse, as his portion; that though the wide universe is full of good, no kernel of nourishing corn can come to him but through his toil bestowed on that plot of ground which is given to him to till. The power which resides in him is new in nature, and none but he knows what that is which he can do, nor does he know until he has tried."

That is the way Emerson said it. But here is the way a poet—the late Douglas Malloch—said it:

> If you can't be a pine on the top of the
> hill,
>   Be a scrub in the valley—but be
> The best little scrub by the side of the
> rill;
>   Be a bush, if you can't be a tree.
>
> If you can't be a bush, be a bit of the
> grass,
>   And some highway happier make;
> If you can't be a muskie, then just be a
> bass—
>   But the liveliest bass in the lake!
>
> We can't all be captains, we've got to
> be crew,
>   There's something for all of us here.
> There's big work to do and there's
> lesser to do
>   And the task we must do is the near.
>
> If you can't be a highway, then just be
> a trail,
>   If you can't be the sun, be a star;

It isn't by size that you win or you
fail—
   Be the best of whatever you are!

To cultivate a mental attitude that will bring us peace and freedom from worry, remember . . .

Let's not imitate others.
Let's find ourselves and be ourselves.

2

Four Good Working Habits That Will Help Prevent Fatigue and Worry

---

GOOD WORKING HABIT NO. 1

Clear Your Desk of All Papers Except Those
Relating to the Immediate Problem at Hand.

Roland L. Williams, President of the Chicago and North-western Railway, once said, "A person with his desk piled high with papers on various matters will find his work much easier and more accurate if he clears that desk of all but the immediate problem on hand. I call this good housekeeping, and it is the number-one step toward efficiency."

If you visit the Library of Congress in Washington, D.C., you will find five words painted on the ceiling—five words written by the poet Pope:

"Order is Heaven's first law."

Order ought to be the first law of business, too. But is it?

No, the average desk is cluttered up with papers that haven't been looked at for weeks. In fact, the publisher of a New Orleans newspaper once told me that his secretary cleared up one of his desks and found a typewriter that had been missing for two years!

The mere sight of a desk littered with unanswered mail and reports and memos is enough to breed confusion, tension, and worries. It is much worse than that. The constant reminder of "a million things to do and no time to do them" can worry you not only into tension and fatigue, but also into high blood pressure, heart trouble, and stomach ulcers.

Dr. John H. Stokes, professor, Graduate School of Medicine, University of Pennsylvania, read a paper before the National Convention of the American Medical Association—a paper entitled "Functional Neuroses as Complications of Organic Disease." In that paper, Dr. Stokes listed eleven conditions under the title: "What to Look for in the Patient's State of Mind." Here is the first item on that list:

> The sense of must or obligation; the unending stretch of things ahead that simply have to be done.

But how can such an elementary procedure as clearing your desk and making decisions help you avoid this high pressure, this sense of *must*, this sense of an "unending stretch of things ahead" that simply have to be done? Dr. William L. Sadler, the famous psychiatrist, told of a patient who, by using this simple device, avoided a nervous breakdown. The man was an executive in a big Chicago firm. When he came to Dr. Sadler's office, he was tense, nervous, worried. He knew he was heading for a tailspin, but he couldn't quit work. He had to have help.

"While this man was telling me his story," Dr. Sadler says, "my telephone rang. It was the hospital calling; and instead of deferring the matter, I took time right then to come to a decision. I always settle questions, if possible, right on the spot. I had no sooner hung up than the phone rang again. Again an urgent matter, which I took time to discuss. The third interruption came when a colleague of mine came to my office for advice on a patient who was critically ill. When I had finished with him, I turned to my caller and began to apologize for keeping him waiting. But he had brightened up. He had a completely different look on his face."

"Don't apologize, doctor!" this man said to Sadler. "In the last ten minutes, I think I've got a hunch as to what is wrong with me. I'm going back to my office and revise my working habits. . . . But before I go, do you mind if I take a look in your desk?"

Dr. Sadler opened up the drawers of his desk. All empty—except for supplies. "Tell me," said the patient, "where do you keep your unfinished business?"

"Finished!" said Sadler.

"And where do you keep your unanswered mail?"

"Answered!" Sadler told him. "My rule is never to lay down a letter until I have answered it. I dictate the reply to my secretary at once."

Six weeks later, this same executive invited Dr. Sadler to come to his office. He was changed—and so was his desk. He opened the desk drawers to show there was no unfinished business inside of the desk. "Six weeks ago," this executive said, "I had three different desks in two different offices—and was snowed under by my work. I was never finished. After talking to you, I came back here and cleared out a wagonload of reports and old papers. Now I work at one desk, settle things as they come up, and don't have a mountain of unfinished business nagging at me and making me tense and worried. But the most astonishing thing is I've recovered completely. There is nothing wrong anymore with my health!"

Charles Evans Hughes, former Chief Justice of the United States Supreme Court, said: "Men do not die from overwork. They die from dissipation and worry." Yes, from dissipation of their energies—and worry because they never seem to get their work done.

GOOD WORKING HABIT NO. 2
Do Things in the Order of Their Importance.

Henry L. Doherty, founder of the nationwide Cities Service Company, said that regardless of how much salary he paid, there were two abilities he found it almost impossible to find.

Those two priceless abilities: first, the ability to think. Second, the ability to do things in the order of their importance.

Charles Luckman, the lad who started from scratch and climbed in twelve years to president of the Pepsodent Company, got a salary of a hundred thousand dollars a year, and made a million dollars besides—that lad declared that he owed much of his success to developing the two abilities that Henry L. Doherty said he found almost impossible to find. Charles Luckman said: "As far back as I can remember, I have gotten up at five o'clock in the morning because I can think better then than any other time—I can think better then and plan my day, plan to do things in the order of their importance."

Frank Bettger, one of America's most successful insurance salesmen, didn't wait until five o'clock in the morning to plan his day. He planned it the night before—set a goal for himself—a goal to sell a certain amount of insurance that day. If he failed, that amount was added to his next day—and so on.

I know from long experience that one is not always able to do things in the order of their importance, but I also know that some kind of plan to do first things first is infinitely better than extemporizing as you go along.

If George Bernard Shaw had not made it a rigid rule to do first things first, he would probably have failed as a writer and might have remained a bank cashier all his life. His plan called for writing five pages each day for nine heart-breaking years, even though he made a total of thirty dollars in those nine years—about a penny a day. Even Robinson Crusoe wrote out a schedule of what he would do each hour of the day.

GOOD WORKING HABIT NO. 3

When You Face a Problem, Solve It Then and There if You Have the Facts Necessary to Make a Decision. Don't Keep Putting Off Decisions.

One of my former students, the late H. P. Howell, told me that when he was a member of the board of directors of U.S. Steel, the meetings of the board were often long-drawn-out affairs—many problems were discussed, few decisions were made. The result: each member of the board had to carry home bundles of reports to study.

Finally, Mr. Howell persuaded the board of directors to take up one problem at a time and come to a decision. No procrastination—no putting off. The decision might be to ask for additional facts; it might be to do something or to do nothing. But a decision was reached on each problem before passing on to the next. Mr. Howell told me that the results were striking and salutary: the docket was cleared.

The calender was clean. No longer was it necessary for each member to carry home a bundle of reports. No longer was there a worried sense of unresolved problems.

A good rule, not only for the board of directors of U.S. Steel, but for you and me.

COOD WORKING HABIT NO. 4
Learn to Organize, Deputize and Supervise.

Many business persons are driving themselves to premature graves because they have never learned to delegate responsibility to others, insisting on doing everything themselves. Result: details and confusion overwhelm them. They are driven by a sense of hurry, worry, anxiety and tension. It is hard to learn to delegate responsibilities. I know. It was hard for me, awfully hard. I also know from experience the disasters that can be caused by delegating authority to the wrong people. But difficult as it is to delegate authority, executives must do it if they are to avoid worry, tension and fatigue.

Executives who build up big businesses and don't learn to organize, deputize and supervise usually pop off with heart trouble in their fifties or early sixties—heart trouble caused by tension and worries. Want a specific instance? Look at the death notices in your local paper.

3

What Makes You Tired—and What You Can Do About It

Here is an astounding and significant fact: Mental work alone can't make you tired. Sounds absurd. But a few years ago, scientists tried to find out how long the human brain could labor without reaching "a diminished capacity for work," the scientific definition of fatigue. To the amazement of these scientists, they discovered that blood passing through the brain, when it is active, shows no fatigue at all! If you took blood from the veins of a day laborer while he was working, you would find it full of "fatigue toxins" and fatigue products. But if you took a drop of blood from the brain of an Albert Einstein, it would show no fatigue toxins whatever at the end of the day.

So far as the brain is concerned, it can work "as well and as swiftly at the end of eight or even twelve hours of effort as at the beginning." The brain is utterly tireless. . . . So what makes you tired?

Psychiatrists declare that most of our fatigue derives from our mental and emotional attitudes. One of England's most distinguished psychiatrists, J. A. Hadfield, says in his book *The Psychology of Power*: "The greater part of the fatigue from which we suffer is of mental origin; in fact exhaustion of purely physical origin is rare."

One of America's most distinguished psychiatrists, Dr. A. A. Brill, goes even further. He declares, "One hundred percent of the fatigue of the sedentary worker in good health is due to psychological factors, by which we mean emotional factors."

What kinds of emotional factors tire the sedentary (or sitting) worker? Joy? Contentment? No! Never! Boredom, resentment, a feeling of not being appreciated, a feeling of futility, hurry, anxiety, worry—those are the emotional factors that exhaust the sitting worker, make him susceptible to colds, reduce his output, and send him home with a nervous headache. Yes, we get tired because our emotions produce nervous tensions in the body.

The Metropolitan Life Insurance Company pointed that out in a leaflet on fatigue: "Hard work by itself," said this great life insurance company, "seldom causes fatigue which cannot be cured by a good sleep or rest. . . . Worry, tenseness, and emotional upsets are three of the biggest causes of fatigue. Often they are to blame when physical or mental work seems to be the cause. . . . Remember that a tense muscle is a working muscle. Ease up! Save energy for important duties."

Stop now, right where you are, and give yourself a checkup. As you read these lines, are you scowling at the book? Do you feel a strain between the eyes? Are you sitting relaxed in your chair? Or are you hunching up your shoulders? Are the muscles of your face tense? Unless your entire body is as limp and relaxed as an old rag doll, you are at this very moment producing nervous tensions and muscular tensions. *You are producing nervous tensions and nervous fatigue!*

Why do we produce these unnecessary tensions in doing mental work? Daniel W. Josselyn said, "I find that the chief obstacle . . . is the almost universal belief that hard work requires a feeling of effort, else it is not well done." So we scowl when we concentrate. We hunch up our shoulders. We call on our muscles to make the motion of *effort*, which in no way assists our brain in its work.

Here is an astonishing and tragic truth: millions of people who wouldn't dream of wasting dollars go right on wasting and squandering their energy with the recklessness of seven drunken sailors in Singapore.

What is the answer to this nervous fatigue? Relax! Relax! Relax! *Learn to relax while you are doing your work!*

Easy? No. You will probably have to reverse the habits of a lifetime. But it is worth the effort, for it may revolutionize your life! William James said, in his essay "The Gospel of Relaxation": "The American overtension and jerkiness and breathlessness and intensity and agony of expression . . . are *bad habits*, nothing more or less." *Tension is a habit. Relaxing is a habit. And bad habits can be broken, good habits formed.*

How do you relax? Do you start with your mind, or do you start with your nerves? You don't start with either. You always begin to *relax with your muscles!*

Let's give it a try. To show how it is done, suppose we start with your eyes. Read this paragraph through, and when you've reached the end, lean back, close your eyes, *and say to your eyes* silently, "Let go. Let go. Stop straining, stop frowning. Let go. Let go." Repeat that over and over very slowly for a minute. . . .

Didn't you notice that after a few seconds the muscles of the eyes *began to obey?* Didn't you feel as though some hand had wiped away the tension? Well, incredible as it seems, you have sampled in that one minute the whole key and secret to the art of relaxing. You can do the same thing with the jaw, with the muscles of the face, with the neck, with the shoulders, the whole of the body. But the most important organ of all is the eye. Dr. Edmund Jacobson of the University of Chicago has gone so far as to say that if you can completely relax the muscles of the eyes, you can forget all your troubles! The reason the eyes are so important in relieving nervous tension is that they burn up one fourth of all the nervous energies consumed by the body. That is also why so many people with perfectly sound vision suffer from "eyestrain." They are tensing the eyes.

Vicki Baum, the famous novelist, said that when she was a child, she met an old man who taught her one of the most important lessons she ever learned. She had fallen down and cut her knees and hurt her wrist. The old man picked her up. He had once been a circus clown, and as he brushed her off, he said, "The reason you injured yourself was because you don't know how to relax. You have to pretend you are as limp as a sock, as an old crumpled sock. Come, I'll show you how to do it."

That old man taught Vicki Baum and the other children how to fall, how to do flip-flops, and how to turn somersaults. And always he insisted, "Think of yourself as an old crumpled sock. Then you've *got* to relax!

You can relax in odd moments, almost anywhere you are. Only don't make an effort to relax. *Relaxation is the absence of all tension and effort*. Think ease and relaxation. Begin by thinking relaxation of the muscles of your eyes and your face, saying over and over, "Let go . . . let go . . . let go and relax." Feel the energy flowing out of your facial muscles to the center of your body. Think of yourself as being as free from tension as a baby.

That is what Galli-Curci, the great soprano, used to do. Helen Jepson told me that she used to see Galli-Curci before a performance, sitting in a chair with all her muscles relaxed and her lower jaw so limp it actually sagged. An excellent practice—it kept her from becoming too nervous before her stage entrance; it prevented fatigue.

Here are four suggestions that will help you learn to relax:

1. Relax in odd moments. Let your body go limp like an old sock. I keep an old, maroon-colored sock on my desk as I work—keep it there as a reminder of how limp I ought to be. If you haven't got a sock, a cat will do. Did you ever pick up a kitten sleeping in the sunshine? If so, both ends sagged like a wet newspaper. Even the yogis in India say that if you want to master the art of relaxation, study the cat. I never saw a tired cat, a cat with a nervous breakdown, or a cat suffering from insomnia, worry, or stomach ulcers. You will probably avoid these disasters if you learn to relax as the cat does.

2. Work, as much as possible, in a comfortable position. Remember that tensions on the body produce aching shoulders and nervous fatigue.

3. Check yourself four or five times a day, and say to yourself, "Am I making my work harder than it actually is? Am I using muscles that have nothing to do with the work I am doing?" This will help you form the *habit* of relaxing, and as Dr. David Harold Fink says, "Among those who know psychology best, it is habits two to one."

4. Test yourself again at the end of the day, by asking yourself, "Just how tired am I? If I am tired, it is not because of the mental work I have done, but the way I have done it." "I measure my accomplishments," said Daniel W. Josselyn, "not by how tired I am at the end of the day, but how tired I am not." He said, "When I feel particularly tired at the end of the day,

or when irritability proves that my nerves are tired, I know beyond question that it has been an inefficient day both as to quantity and quality." If every businessperson in America would learn that same lesson, our death rate from "hypertension" diseases would drop overnight. And we would stop filling up our sanitariums and asylums with people who have been broken by fatigue and worry.

4

How to Banish the Boredom That Produces Fatigue, Worry and Resentment

One of the chief causes of fatigue is boredom. To illustrate, let's take the case of Alice, an executive who lives on your street. Alice came home one night utterly exhausted. She *acted* fatigued. She *was* fatigued. She had a headache. She had a backache. She was so exhausted she wanted to go to bed without waiting for dinner. Her mother pleaded. . . . She sat down at the table. The telephone rang. The boy friend! An invitation to a dance! Her eyes sparkled. Her spirits soared. She rushed upstairs, put on her Alice-Blue gown, and danced until three o'clock in the morning; and when she finally did get home, she was not the slightest bit exhausted. She was, in fact, so exhilarated she couldn't fall asleep.

Was Alice really and honestly tired eight hours earlier, when she looked and acted exhausted? Sure she was. She was exhausted because she was bored with her work, perhaps bored with life. There are millions of Alices. You may be one of them.

It is a well-known fact that your emotional attitude usually has far more to do with producing fatigue than has physical exertion. A few years ago, Joseph E. Barmack, Ph.D., published in the *Archives of Psychology* a report of some of his experiments, showing how boredom produces fatigue. Dr. Barmack put a group of students through a series of tests in which, he knew, they could have little interest. The result? The students felt tired and sleepy, complained of headaches and eyestrain, felt irritable. In some cases, even their stomachs were upset. Was it all "imagination"? No. Metabolism tests were taken of these students. These tests showed that the blood pressure of the body and the consumption of oxygen actually decrease when a person is bored, and that the whole metabolism picks up immediately as soon as he begins to feel interest and pleasure in his work!

We rarely get tired when we are doing something interesting and exciting. For example, I recently took a vacation in the Canadian Rockies up around Lake Louise. I spent several days trout fishing along Corral Creek, fighting my way through brush higher than my head, stumbling over logs, struggling through fallen timber—yet after eight hours of this, I was not exhausted. Why? Because I was excited, exhilarated. I had a sense of high achievement: six cutthroat trout. But suppose I had been bored by fishing, then how do you think I would have felt? I would have been worn out by such strenuous work at an altitude of seven thousand feet.

Even in such exhausting activities as mountain climbing, boredom may tire you far more than the strenuous work involved. For example, Mr. S. H. Kingman, president of the Farmers and Mechanics Savings Bank of Minneapolis, told me of an incident that is a perfect illustration of that statement. In July, 1953, the Canadian government asked the Canadian Alpine Club to furnish guides to train the members of the Prince of Wales Rangers in mountain climbing. Mr. Kingman was one of the guides chosen to train these soldiers. He told me how he and the other guides—men ranging from forty-two to fifty-nine years of age—took these young army men on long hikes across glaciers and snow fields and up a sheer cliff of forty feet, where they had to climb with ropes and tiny footholds and precarious handholds. They climbed Michael's Peak, the Vice-President Peak, and other unnamed peaks in the Little Yoho Valley in the Canadian Rockies. After fifteen hours of mountain climbing, these young men, who were in the pink of condition (they had just finished a six-week course in tough Commando training), were utterly exhausted.

Was their fatigue caused by using muscles that had not been hardened by Commando training? Anyone who had ever been through Commando training would hoot at such a ridiculous question! No, they were utterly exhausted because they were bored by mountain climbing. They were so tired that many of them fell asleep without waiting to eat. But the guides—men who were two and three times as old as the soldiers—were they tired? Yes, but not exhausted. The guides ate dinner and stayed up for hours, talking about the day's experiences. They were not exhausted because they were interested.

When Dr. Edward Thorndike of Columbia was conducting experiments in fatigue, he kept young men awake for almost a week by keeping them constantly interested. After much investigation, Dr. Thorndike is reported to have said: "Boredom is the only real cause of diminution of work."

If you are a mental worker, it is seldom the amount of work you do that makes you tired. You may be tired by the amount of work you do *not* do. For example, remember the day last week when you were constantly interrupted. No letters answered. Appointments broken. Trouble here and there. Everything went wrong that day. You accomplished nothing whatever, yet you went home exhausted—and with a splitting head.

The next day everything clicked at the office. You accomplished forty times more than you did the previous day. Yet you went home fresh as a snowy-white gardenia. You have had that experience. So have I.

The lesson to be learned? Just this: our fatigue is often caused not by work, but by worry, frustration, and resentment.

While writing this chapter, I went to see a revival of Jerome Kern's delightful musical comedy *Show Boat*. Captain Andy, captain of the *Cotton Blossom*, says in one of his philosophical interludes: "The lucky folks are the ones that get to do things they enjoy doing." Such folk are lucky because they have more energy, more happiness, less worry and less fatigue. Where your interests are, there is your energy also. Walking ten blocks with a nagging wife or husband can be more fatiguing than walking ten miles with an adoring sweetheart.

And so what? What can you do about it? Well, here is what one stenographer did about it—a stenographer working for an oil company in Tulsa, Oklahoma. For several days each month, she had one of the dullest jobs imaginable: filling out printed forms for oil leases, inserting figures and statistics. This task was so boring that she resolved, in self-defense, to make it interesting. How? She had a daily contest with herself. She counted the number of forms she filled out each morning, and then tried to excel that record in the afternoon. She counted each day's total and tried to better it the next day. Result? She was soon able to fill out more of these dull printed forms than any other stenographer in her division. And what did all this get her? Praise? No. . . . Thanks? No. . . . Promotion? No. . . . Increased pay? No. . . . But it did help to prevent the fatigue that is spawned by boredom. It did give her a mental stimulant. Because she had done her best to make a dull job interesting, she had more energy, more zest, and got far more happiness out of her leisure hours.

I happen to know this story is true, because I married that girl.

Here is the story of another stenographer who found it paid to act *as if* her work were interesting. She used to fight her work. But no more. She is Miss Vallie G. Golden, of Elmhurst, Illinois. Here is her story, as she wrote it to me:

"There are four stenographers in my office and each of us is assigned to take letters from several men. Once in a while we get jammed up in these assignments. One day, when an assistant department head insisted that I do a long letter over, I started to rebel. I tried to point out to him that the letter could be corrected without being retyped—and he retorted that if I didn't do it over, he would find someone else who would! I was absolutely fuming! But as I started to retype this letter, it suddenly occurred to me that there were a lot of other people who would jump at the chance to do the work I was doing. Also, that I was being paid a salary to do just that work. I began to feel better. I suddenly made up my mind to do my work as if I actually enjoyed it—even though I despised it. Then I made this important discovery: if I do my work *as if* I really enjoy it, then I do enjoy it to some extent. I also found I can work faster when I enjoy my work. So there is seldom any need now for me to work overtime. This new attitude of mine gained me the reputation of being a good worker. And when one of the department superintendents needed a private secretary, he asked for me for the job—because, he said, I was willing to do extra work without being sulky! This matter of the power of a changed mental attitude," wrote Miss Golden, "has been a tremendously important discovery to me. It has worked wonders!"

Miss Golden used the wonder-working "*as if*" philosophy of Professor Hans Vaihinger. He taught us to act "*as if*" we were happy—and so on.

If you act "*as if*" you are interested in your job, that bit of acting will tend to make your interest real. It will also tend to decrease your fatigue, your tensions, and your worries.

A few years ago, Harlan A. Howard made a decision that completely altered his life. He resolved to make a dull job interesting—and he certainly had a dull one: washing plates, scrubbing counters, and dishing out ice cream in the high-school lunchroom while the other boys were playing ball or kidding the girls. Harlan Howard despised his job—but since he had to stick to it, he resolved to study ice cream—how it was made, what ingredients were used, why some ice creams were better than others. He studied the chemistry of ice cream, and became a whiz in the high-school chemistry course. He was so interested now in food chemistry that he entered the Massachusetts State College and majored in the field of "food technology." When the New York Cocoa Exchange offered a hundred-dollar prize for the best paper on uses of cocoa and chocolate—a prize open to all college students—who do you suppose won it? . . . That's right. Harlan Howard.

When he found it difficult to get a job, he opened a private laboratory in the basement of his home in Amherst, Massachusetts. Shortly after that, a new law was passed. The bacteria in milk had to be counted. Harlan A. Howard was soon counting bacteria for the fourteen milk companies in Amherst—and he had to hire two assistants.

Where will he be twenty-five years from now? Well, the

men who are now running the business of food chemistry will be retired then, or dead; and their places will be taken by young lads who are now radiating initiative and enthusiasm. Twenty-five years from now, Harlan A. Howard will probably be one of the leaders in his profession, while some of his classmates to whom he used to sell ice cream over the counter will be sour, unemployed, cussing the government, and complaining that they never had a chance. Harlan A. Howard might never have had a chance, either, if he hadn't resolved to make a dull job interesting.

Years ago, there was another young man who was bored with his dull job of standing at a lathe, turning out bolts in a factory. His first name was Sam. Sam wanted to quit, but he was afraid he couldn't find another job. Since he had to do this dull work, Sam decided he would make it interesting. So he ran a race with the mechanic operating a machine beside him. One of them was to trim off the rough surfaces on his machine, and the other was to trim the bolts down to the proper diameter. They would switch machines occasionally and see who could turn out the most bolts. The foreman, impressed with Sam's speed and accuracy, soon gave him a better job. That was the start of a whole series of promotions. Thirty years later, Sam—Samuel Vauclain—was president of the Baldwin Locomotive Works. But he might have remained a mechanic all his life if he had not resolved to make a dull job interesting.

H. V. Kaltenborn—the famous radio news analyst—once told me how he made a dull job interesting. When he was twenty-two years old, he worked his way across the Atlantic on a cattle boat, feeding and watering the steers. After making a bicycle tour of England, he arrived in Paris, hungry and broke. Pawning his camera for five dollars, he put an ad in the Paris edition of *The New York Herald* and got a job selling stereopticon machines. I can remember those old-fashioned stereoscopes that we used to hold up before our eyes to look at two pictures exactly alike. As we looked, a miracle happened. The two lenses in the stereoscope transformed the two pictures into a single scene with the effect of a third dimension. We saw distance. We got an astounding sense of perspective.

Well, as I was saying, Kaltenborn started out selling these machines from door to door in Paris—and he couldn't speak French. But he earned five thousand dollars in commissions the first year, and made himself one of the highest-paid salesmen in France that year. H. V. Kaltenborn told me that this experience did as much to develop within him the qualities that make for success as did any single year of study at Harvard. Confidence? He told me himself that after that experience, he felt he could have sold *The Congressional Record* to French housewives.

That experience gave him an intimate understanding of French life that later proved invaluable in interpreting, on the radio, European events.

How did he manage to become an expert salesman when he couldn't speak French? Well, he had his employer write out his sales talk in perfect French, and he memorized it. He would ring a doorbell, a housewife would answer, and Kaltenborn would begin repeating his memorized sales talk with an accent so terrible it was funny. He would show the housewife his pictures, and when she asked a question, he would shrug his shoulders and say, "An American . . . an American." He would then take off his hat and point to a copy of the sales talk in perfect French that he had pasted in the top of his hat. The housewife would laugh, he would laugh—and show her more pictures. When H. V. Kaltenborn told me about this, he confessed that the job had been far from easy. He told me that there was only one quality that pulled him through: his determination to make the job interesting. Every morning before he started out, he looked into the mirror and gave himself a pep talk: *"Kaltenborn, you have to do this if you want to eat. Since you have to do it—why not have a good time doing it? Why not imagine every time you ring a doorbell that you are an actor before the footlights and that there's an audience out there looking at you? After all, what you are doing is just as funny as something on the stage. So why not put a lot of zest and enthusiasm into it?"*

Mr. Kaltenborn told me that these daily pep talks helped him transform a task that he had once hated and dreaded into an adventure that he liked and made highly profitable.

When I asked Mr. Kaltenborn if he had any advice to give to the young men of America who are eager to succeed, he said: "Yes, go to bat with yourself every morning. We talk a lot about the importance of physical exercise to wake us up out of the half-sleep in which so many of us walk around. But we need, even more, some spiritual and mental exercises every morning to stir us into action. Give yourself a pep talk every day."

Is giving yourself a pep talk every day silly, superficial, childish? No, on the contrary, it is the very essence of sound psychology. "Our life is what our thoughts make it." These words are just as true today as they were eighteen centuries ago when Marcus Aurelius first wrote them in his book on *Meditations:* "Our life is what our thoughts make it."

By talking to yourself every hour of the day, you can direct yourself to think thoughts of courage and happiness, thoughts of power and peace. By talking to yourself about the things you have to be grateful for, you can fill your mind with thoughts that soar and sing.

By thinking the right thoughts, you can make any job less distasteful. Your boss wants you to be interested in your job so that he or she will make more money. But let's forget about what the boss wants. Think only of what getting interested in your job will do for you. Remind yourself that it may double the amount of happiness you get out of life, for you spend about one half of your waking hours at your work, and if you don't find happiness in your work, you may never find it anywhere. Keep reminding yourself that getting interested in your job will take your mind off your worries, and, in the long run, will probably bring promotion and increased pay. Even if it doesn't do that, it will reduce fatigue to a minimum and help you enjoy your hours of leisure.

5

Would You Take a Million Dollars for What You Have?

I have known Harold Abbott for years. He lived in Webb City, Missouri. He used to be my lecture manager. One day he and I met in Kansas City and he drove me down to my farm at Belton, Missouri. During that drive, I asked him how he kept from worrying; and he told me an inspiring story that I shall never forget.

"I used to worry a lot," he said, "but one spring day in 1934, I was walking down West Dougherty Street in Webb City when I saw a sight that banished all my worries. It all happened in ten seconds, but during those ten seconds I learned more about how to live than I had learned in the previous ten years. For two years I had been running a grocery store in Webb City," Harold Abbott said, as he told me the story. "I had not only lost all my savings, but I had incurred debts that took me seven years to pay back. My grocery store had been closed the previous Saturday; and now I was going to the Merchants and Miners Bank to borrow money so I could go to Kansas City to look for a job. I walked like a beaten man. I had lost all my fight and faith. Then suddenly I saw coming down the street a man who had no legs. He was sitting on a little wooden platform equipped with wheels from roller skates. He propelled himself along the street with a block of wood in each hand. I met him just after he had crossed the street and was starting to lift himself up a few inches over the curb to the sidewalk. As he tilted his little wooden platform to an angle, his eyes met mine. He greeted me with a grand smile. 'Good morning, sir. It is a fine morning, isn't it?' he said with spirit. As I stood looking at him, I realized how rich I was. I had two legs. I could walk. I felt ashamed of my self-pity. I said to myself, if he can be happy, cheerful, and confident without legs, I certainly can with legs. I could already feel my chest lifting. I had intended to ask the Merchants and Miners Bank for only one hundred dollars. But now I had courage to ask for *two* hundred. I had intended to say that I wanted to go to Kansas City to *try* to get a job. But now I announced confidently that I wanted to go to Kansas City to *get* a job. I got the loan; and I got the job.

"I now have the following words pasted on my bathroom mirror, and I read them every morning as I shave:

> *I had the blues because I had no shoes,*
> *Until upon the street, I met a man who had no feet."*

I once asked Eddie Rickenbacker what was the biggest lesson he had learned from drifting about with his companions in life rafts for twenty-one days, hopelessly lost in the Pacific. "The biggest lesson I learned from that experience," he said, "was that if you have all the fresh water you want to drink and all the food you want to eat, you ought never to complain about anything."

Time ran an article about a sergeant who had been wounded on Guadalcanal. Hit in the throat by a shell fragment, this sergeant had had seven blood transfusions. Writing a note to his doctor, he asked: "Will I live?" The doctor replied: "Yes." He wrote another note, asking, "Will I be able to talk?" Again the answer was yes. He then wrote another note, saying: *"Then what in the hell am I worrying about?"*

Why don't you stop right now and ask yourself, "What in the hell am I worrying about?" You will probably find that it is comparatively unimportant and insignificant.

About ninety percent of the things in our lives are right and about ten percent are wrong. If we want to be happy, all we have to do is to concentrate on the ninety percent that are right and ignore the ten percent that are wrong. If we want to be worried and bitter and have stomach ulcers, all we have to do is to concentrate on the ten percent that are wrong and ignore the ninety percent that are glorious.

The words "Think and Thank" are inscribed in many of the Cromwellian churches of England. These words ought to be inscribed on our hearts, too: "Think and Thank." Think of all we have to be grateful for, and thank God for all our boons and bounties.

Jonathan Swift, author of *Gulliver's Travels*, was the most devastating pessimist in English literature. He was so sorry that he had been born that he wore black and fasted on his birthdays; yet, in his despair, this supreme pessimist of English literature praised the great health-giving powers of cheerfulness and happiness. "The best doctors in the world," he declared, "are Doctor Diet, Doctor Quiet, and Doctor Merryman."

You and I may have the services of "Doctor Merryman" free every day by keeping our attention fixed on all the incredible riches we possess—riches exceeding by far the fabled treasures of Ali Baba. Would you sell both your eyes for a billion dollars? What would you take for your two legs? Your hands? Your hearing? Your children? Your family? Add up your assets, and you will find that you won't sell what you have for all the gold ever amassed by the Rockefellers, the Fords, and the Morgans combined.

But do we appreciate all this? Ah, no. As Schopenhauer said: "We seldom think of what we have but always of what we lack." Yes, the tendency to "seldom think of what we have but always of what we lack" is the greatest tragedy on earth. It has probably caused more misery than all the wars and diseases in history.

It caused John Palmer to turn "from a regular guy into an old grouch," and almost wrecked his home. I know because he told me so.

Mr. Palmer lived in Paterson, New Jersey. "Shortly after I returned from the Army," he said, "I started in business for myself. I worked hard day and night. Things were going nicely. Then trouble started. I couldn't get parts and materials. I was afraid I would have to give up my business. I worried so much that I changed from a regular guy into an old grouch. I became so sour and cross that— well, I didn't know it then but I now realize that I came very near to losing my happy home. Then one day a young, disabled veteran who works for me said, 'Johnny, you ought to be ashamed of yourself. You take on as if you were the only person in the world with troubles. Suppose you do have to shut up shop for a while—so what? You can start up again when things get normal. You've got a lot to be thankful for. Yet you are always growling. Boy, how I wish I were in your shoes! Look at me. I've got only one arm, and half of my face is shot away, and yet I am not complaining: If you don't stop your growling and grumbling, you will lose not only your business, but also your health, your home, and your friends!'

"Those remarks stopped me dead in my tracks. They made me realize how well off I was. I resolved then and there that I would change and be my old self again—and I did."

A friend of mine, Lucile Blake, had to tremble on the

edge of tragedy before she learned to be happy about what she had instead of worrying over what she lacked.

I met Lucile years ago, when we were both studying short-story writing in the Columbia University School of Journalism. Some years ago, she got the shock of her life. She was living then in Tucson, Arizona. She had—well, here is the story as she told it to me:

"I had been living in a whirl: studying the organ at the University of Arizona, conducting a speech clinic in town, and teaching a class in musical appreciation at the Desert Willow Ranch, where I was staying. I was going in for parties, dances, horseback rides under the stars. One morning I collapsed. My heart! 'You will have to lie in bed for a year of complete rest,' the doctor said. He didn't encourage me to believe I would ever be strong again.

"In bed for a year! To be an invalid—perhaps to die! I was terror-stricken! Why did all this have to happen to me? What had I done to deserve it? I wept and wailed. I was bitter and rebellious. But I did go to bed as the doctor advised. A neighbor of mine, Mr. Rudolf, an artist, said to me, 'You think now that spending a year in bed will be a tragedy. But it won't be. You will have time to think and get acquainted with yourself. You will make more spiritual growth in these next few months than you have made during all your previous life.' I became calmer, and tried to develop a new sense of values. I read books of inspiration. One day I heard a radio commentator say: 'You can express only what is in your own consciousness.' I had heard words like these many times before, but now they reached down inside me and took root. I resolved to think only the thoughts I wanted to live by: thoughts of joy, happiness, health. I forced myself each morning, as soon as I awoke, to go over all the things I had to be grateful for. No pain. A lovely young daughter. My eyesight. My hearing. Lovely music on the radio. Time to read. Good food. Good friends.

I was so cheerful and had so many visitors that the doctor put up a sign saying that only one visitor at a time would be allowed in my cabin—and only at certain hours.

"Many years have passed since then, and I now lead a full, active life. I am deeply grateful now for that year I spent in bed. It was the most valuable and the happiest year I spent in Arizona. The habit I formed then of counting my blessings each morning still remains with me. It is one of my most precious possessions. I am ashamed to realize that I never really learned to live until I feared I was going to die."

My dear Lucile Blake, you may not realize it, but you learned the same lesson that Dr. Samuel Johnson learned two hundred years ago. "The habit of looking on the best side of every event," said Dr. Johnson, "is worth more than a thousand pounds a year."

Those words were uttered, mind you, not by a professional optimist, but by a man who had known anxiety, rags, and hunger for twenty years—and finally became one of the most eminent writers of his generation and the most celebrated conversationalist of all time.

Logan Pearsall Smith packed a lot of wisdom into a few words when he said: "There are two things to aim at in life: first, to get what you want; and, after that, to enjoy it. Only the wisest of mankind achieve the second."

Would you like to know how to make even dishwashing at the kitchen sink a thrilling experience? If so, read an inspiring book of incredible courage by Borghild Dahl. It is called *I Wanted to See.*

This book was written by a woman who was practically blind for half a century. "I had only one eye," she writes, "and it was so covered with dense scars that I had to do all my seeing through one small opening in the left of the eye. I could see a book only by holding it up close to my face and by straining my one eye as hard as I could to the left."

But she refused to be pitied, refused to be considered "different." As a child, she wanted to play hopscotch with other children, but she couldn't see the markings. So after the other children had gone home, she got down on the ground and crawled along with her eyes near the marks. She memorized every bit of the ground where she and her friends played and soon became an expert at running games. She did her reading at home, holding a book of large print so close to her eyes that her eyelashes brushed the pages. She earned two college degrees: an A.B. from the University of Minnesota and a Master of Arts from Columbia University.

She started teaching in the tiny village of Twin Valley, Minnesota, and rose until she became professor of journalism and literature at Augustana College in Sioux Falls, South Dakota. She taught there for thirteen years, lecturing before women's clubs and giving radio talks about books and authors. "In the back of my mind," she writes, "there had always lurked a fear of total blindness. In order to overcome this, I had adopted a cheerful, almost hilarious, attitude toward life."

Then in 1943, when she was fifty-two years old, a miracle happened: an operation at the famous Mayo Clinic. She could now see forty times as well as she had ever been able to see before.

A new and exciting world of loveliness opened before her. She now found it thrilling even to wash dishes in the kitchen sink. "I begin to play with the white fluffy suds in the dishpan," she writes. "I dip my hands into them and I pick up a ball of tiny soap bubbles. I hold them up against the light, and in each of them I can see the brilliant colors of a miniature rainbow."

As she looked through the window above the kitchen sink, she saw "the flapping gray-black wings of the sparrows flying through the thick, falling snow."

She found such ecstasy looking at the soap bubbles and sparrows that she closed her book with these words: " 'Dear Lord,' I whisper, 'Our Father in Heaven, I thank Thee. I thank Thee.' "

Imagine thanking God because you can wash dishes and see rainbows in bubbles and sparrows flying through the snow!

You and I ought to be ashamed of ourselves. All the days of our years we have been living in a fairyland of beauty, but we have been too blind to see, too satiated to enjoy.

If you want to stop worrying and start living, remember . . .

Count your blessings—not your troubles!

6

Remember That No One Ever Kicks a Dead Dog

An event occurred in 1929 that created a national sensation in educational circles. Learned men from all over America rushed to Chicago to witness the affair. A few years earlier, a young man by the name of Robert Hutchins had worked his way through Yale, acting as a waiter, a lumberjack, a tutor, and a clothesline salesman. Now, only eight years later, he was being inaugurated as president of the fourth-richest university in America, the University of Chicago. His age? Thirty. Incredible! The older educators shook their heads. Criticism came roaring down upon this "boy wonder" like a rockslide. He was this and he was that—too young, inexperienced—his educational ideas were cock-eyed. Even the newspapers joined in the attack.

The day he was inaugurated, a friend said to the father of Robert Maynard Hutchins: "I was shocked this morning to read that newspaper editorial denouncing your son."

"Yes," the elder Hutchins replied, "it was severe, but remember that no one ever kicks a dead dog."

Yes, and the more important a dog is, the more satisfaction people get in kicking him. The Prince of Wales, who later became Edward VIII, had that brought home to him in the seat of his pants. He was attending Dartmouth College in Devonshire at the time—a college that corresponds to our Naval Academy in Annapolis. The Prince was about fourteen. One day one of the naval officers found him crying, and asked him what was wrong. He refused to tell at first, but finally admitted the truth: he was being kicked by the naval cadets. The commodore of the college summoned the boys and explained to them that the Prince had not complained, but he wanted to find out why the Prince had been singled out for this rough treatment.

After much hemming and hawing and toe scraping, the cadets finally confessed that when they themselves became commanders and captains in the King's navy, they wanted to be able to say that they had kicked the King!

So when you are kicked and criticized, remember that it is often done because it gives the kicker a feeling of importance. It often means that you are accomplishing something and are worthy of attention. Many people get a sense of savage satisfaction out of denouncing those who are better educated than they are or more successful. For example, while I was writing this chapter, I received a letter from a woman denouncing General William Booth, founder of the Salvation Army. I had given a laudatory broadcast about General Booth; so this woman wrote me, saying that General Booth had stolen eight million dollars of the money he had collected to help poor people. The charge, of course, was absurd. But this woman wasn't looking for truth. She was seeking the mean-spirited gratification that she got from tearing down someone far above her. I threw her bitter letter into the wastebasket, and thanked Almighty God that I wasn't married to her. Her letter didn't tell me anything at all about General Booth, but it did tell me a lot about her. Schopenhauer had said it years ago: "Vulgar people take huge delight in the faults and follies of great men."

One hardly thinks of the president of Yale as a vulgar man; yet a former president of Yale, Timothy Dwight, apparently took huge delight in denouncing a man who was running for president of the United States. The president of Yale warned that if this man were elected president, "We may see our wives and daughters the victims of legal prostitution, soberly dishonored, speciously polluted; the outcasts of delicacy and virtue, the loathing of God and man."

Sounds almost like a denunciation of Hitler, doesn't it? But it wasn't. It was a denunciation of Thomas Jefferson. *Which* Thomas Jefferson? Surely not the *immortal* Thomas Jefferson, the author of the Declaration of Independence, the patron saint of democracy? Yes, verily, that was the man.

What American do you suppose was denounced as a "hypocrite," "an imposter," and as "little better than a murderer"? A newspaper cartoon depicted him on a guillotine, the big knife ready to cut off his head. Crowds jeered at him and hissed him as he rode through the streets. Who was he? George Washington.

But that occurred a long time ago. Maybe human nature has improved since then. Let's see. Let's take the case of Admiral Peary, the explorer who startled and thrilled the world by reaching the North Pole with dog sleds on April 6, 1909—a goal that brave men for centuries had suffered and starved and died to attain. Peary himself almost died from cold and starvation; and eight of his toes were frozen so hard they had to be cut off. He was so overwhelmed with disasters that he feared he would go insane. His superior naval officers in Washington were burned up because Peary was getting so much publicity and acclaim. So they accused him of collecting money for scientific expeditions and then "lying around and loafing in the Arctic." And they probably believed it, because it is almost impossible not to believe what you want to believe. Their determination to humiliate and block Peary was so violent that only a direct order from President McKinley enabled Peary to continue his career in the Arctic.

Would Peary have been denounced if he had had a desk job in the Navy Department in Washington? No. He wouldn't have been important enough then to have aroused jealousy.

General Grant had an even worse experience than Admiral Peary. In 1862, General Grant won the first great victory that the North had enjoyed—a victory that was achieved in one afternoon, a victory that made Grant a national idol overnight, a victory that had tremendous repercussions even in far-off Europe, a victory that set church bells ringing and bonfires blazing from Maine to the banks of the Mississippi. Yet within six weeks after achieving that great victory, Grant—hero of the North— was *arrested and his army was taken from him. He wept with humiliation and despair.*

Why was General U. S. Grant arrested at the flood tide of his victory? Largely because he had aroused the jealousy and envy of his arrogant superiors.

If we are tempted to be worried about unjust criticism . . .

Remember that unjust criticism is often a disguised compliment. Remember that no one ever kicks a dead dog.

7

Do This—and Criticism Can't Hurt You

I once interviewed Major General Smedley Butler—old "Gimlet-Eye." Old "Hell-Devil" Butler! Remember him? One of the most colorful, swashbuckling generals who ever commanded the United States Marines.

He told me that when he was young, he was desperately eager to be popular, wanted to make a good impression on everyone. In those days the slightest criticism smarted and stung. But he confessed that thirty years in the Marines had toughened his hide. "I have been berated and insulted," he said, "and denounced as a yellow dog, a snake, and a skunk. I have been cursed by the experts. I have been called every possible combination of unprintable. cuss words in the English language. Bother me? Huh! When I hear somebody cussing me now, I never turn my head to see who is talking."

Maybe old "Gimlet-Eye" Butler was too indifferent to criticism; but one thing is sure: most of us take the little jibes and javelins that are hurled at us far too seriously. I remember the time, years ago, when a reporter from the New York *Sun* attended a demonstration meeting of my adult-education classes and lampooned me and my work. Was I burned up? I took it as a personal insult. I telephoned Gil Hodges, the chairman of the Executive Committee of the *Sun*, and practically demanded that he print an article stating the facts—instead of ridicule. I was determined to make the punishment fit the crime.

I am ashamed now of the way I acted. I realize now that half the people who bought the paper never saw that article. Half of those who read it regarded it as a source of innocent merriment. Half of those who gloated over it forgot all about it in a few weeks.

I realize now that people are not thinking about you and me or caring what is said about us. They are thinking about themselves—before breakfast, after breakfast, and right on until ten minutes past midnight. They would be a thousand times more concerned about a slight headache of their own than they would about the news of your death or mine.

Even if you and I are lied about, ridiculed, double-crossed, knifed in the back, and sold down the river by one out of every six of our most intimate friends—let's not indulge in an orgy of self-pity. Instead, let's remind ourselves that that's precisely what happened to Jesus. One of His twelve most intimate friends turned traitor for a bribe that would amount, in our modern money, to about nineteen dollars. Another one of His twelve most intimate friends openly deserted Jesus the moment He got into trouble, and declared three times that he didn't even know Jesus—and swore as he said it. One out of six! That is what happened to Jesus. Why should you and I expect a better score?

I discovered years ago that although I couldn't keep people from criticizing me unjustly, I could do something infinitely more important: I could determine whether I would let the unjust condemnation disturb me.

Let's be clear about this: I am not advocating ignoring

all criticism. Far from it. I am talking about *ignoring only unjust criticism*. I once asked Eleanor Roosevelt how she handled unjust criticism—and Allah knows she had a lot of it. She probably had more ardent friends and more violent enemies than any other woman who ever lived in the White House.

She told me that as a young girl she was almost morbidly shy, afraid of what people might say. She was so afraid of criticism that one day she asked her aunt, Theodore Roosevelt's sister, for advice. She said: "Auntie Bye, I want to do so-and-so. But I'm afraid of being criticized."

Teddy Roosevelt's sister looked her in the eye and said: "Never be bothered by what people say, as long as you know in your heart you are right." Eleanor Roosevelt told me that that bit of advice proved to be her Rock of Gibraltar years later, when she was in the White House. She told me that the only way we can avoid all criticism is to be like a Dresden-china figure and stay on a shelf. "Do what you feel in your heart to be right—for you'll be criticized, anyway. You'll be 'damned if you do, and damned if you don't.' " That is her advice.

When the late Matthew C. Brush was president of the American International Corporation, I asked him if he was ever sensitive to criticism; and he replied, "Yes, I was very sensitive to it in my early days. I was eager then to have all the employees in the organization think I was perfect. If they didn't, it worried me. I would try to please first one person who had been sounding off against me; but the very thing I did to patch it up with him would make someone else mad. Then when I tried to fix it up with this person, I would stir up a couple of other bumblebees. I finally discovered that the more I tried to pacify and to smooth over injured feelings in order to escape personal criticism, the more certain I was to increase my enemies. So finally I said to myself, 'If you get your head above the crowd, you're going to be criticized. So get used to the idea.' That helped me tremendously. From that time on I made it a rule to do the very best I could and then put up my old umbrella and let the rain of criticism drain off me instead of run down my neck."

Deems Taylor went a bit further: he let the rain of criticism run down his neck and had a good laugh over it—in public. When he was giving his comments during the intermission of the Sunday-afternoon radio concerts of the New York Philharmonic-Symphony Orchestra, one woman wrote him a letter calling him "a liar, a traitor, a snake, and a moron." Mr. Taylor says in his book, *Of Men and Music:* "I have a suspicion that she didn't care for that talk." On the following week's broadcast, Mr. Taylor read this letter ove the radio to millions of listeners—and received another letter from the same lady a few days later, "expressing her unaltered opinion," says Mr. Taylor, "that I was *still* a liar, a traitor, a snake, and a moron." We can't keep from admiring a man who takes criticism like that. We admire his serenity, his unshaken poise, and his sense of humor.

When Charles Schwab was addressing the student body at Princeton, he confessed that one of the most important lessons he had ever learned was taught to him by an old German who worked in Schwab's steel mill. This old German got involved in a hot wartime argument with the other steelworkers, and they tossed him into the river. "When he came into my office," Mr. Schwab said, "covered with mud and water, I asked him what he had said to the men who had thrown him into the river, and he replied, 'I just laughed.' "

Mr. Schwab declared that he had adopted that old German's words as his motto: "Just laugh."

That motto is especially good when you are the victim of unjust criticism. You can answer the man who answers you back, but what can you say to the man who "just laughs"?

Lincoln might have broken under the strain of the Civil

War if he hadn't learned the folly of trying to answer all the vitriolic condemnations hurled at him. His description of how he handled his critics has become a literary gem—a classic. General MacArthur had a copy of it hanging above his headquarters desk during the war; and Winston Churchill had a framed copy of it on the wall of his study at Chartwell. It goes like this: "If I were to try to read, much less to answer, all the attacks made on me, this shop might as well be closed for any other business. I do the very best I know how—the very best I can; and I mean to keep on doing so until the end. If the end brings me out all right, then what is said against me won't matter. If the end brings me out wrong, then ten angels swearing I was right would make no difference."

When you and I are unjustly criticized, let's remember to:

> Do the very best you can; and then
> put up your old umbrella and keep the
> rain of criticism from running down
> the back of your neck.

PART TWO

FUNDAMENTAL TECHNIQUES IN HANDLING PEOPLE

How to Win Friends and Influence People is a book on human relations—on getting along with people, on the need for friends in living a full life. Resisting the temptation to criticize and getting in the habit of giving praise and honest appreciation will do more than anything else to make people like us. And the same things that make us happy in the world will give us a happy home life too—the first need of every man and woman.

8

"If You Want to Gather Honey, Don't Kick Over the Beehive"

On May 7, 1931, the most sensational manhunt New York City had ever known had come to its climax. After weeks of search, "Two Gun" Crowley—the killer, the gunman who didn't smoke or drink—was at bay, trapped in his sweetheart's apartment on West End Avenue.

One hundred and fifty policemen and detectives laid siege to his top-floor hideaway. They chopped holes in the roof; they tried to smoke out Crowley, the "cop killer," with teargas. Then they mounted their machine guns on surrounding buildings, and for more than an hour one of New York's fine residential areas reverberated with the crack of pistol fire and the *rat-tat-tat* of machine guns. Crowley, crouching behind an overstuffed chair, fired incessantly at the police. Ten thousand excited people watched the battle. Nothing like it had ever been seen before on the sidewalks of New York.

When Crowley was captured, Police Commissioner

E. P. Mulrooney declared that the two-gun desperado was one of the most dangerous criminals ever encountered in the history of New York. "He will kill," said the commissioner, "at the drop of a feather."

But how did "Two Gun" Crowley regard himself? We know, because while the police were firing into the apartment, he wrote a letter addressed "To whom it may concern." And, as he wrote, the blood flowing from his wounds left a crimson trail on the paper. In this letter Crowley said: "Under my coat is a weary heart, but a kind one—one that would do nobody any harm."

A short time before this, Crowley had been having a necking party with his girl friend on a country road out on Long Island. Suddenly a policemen walked up to the car and said: "Let me see your license."

Without saying a word, Crowley drew his gun and cut the policeman down with a shower of lead. As the dying officer fell, Crowley leaped out of the car, grabbed the officer's revolver, and fired another bullet into the prostrate body. And that was the killer who said: "Under my coat is a weary heart, but a kind one—one that would do nobody any harm."

Crowley was sentenced to the electric chair. When he arrived at the death house in ing Sing, did he say, "This is what I get for killing people?" No, he said: "This is what I get for defending myself."

The point of the story is this: "Two Gun" Crowley didn't blame himself for anything.

Is that an unusual attitude among criminals? If you think so, listen to this:

"I have spent the best years of my life giving people the lighter pleasures, helping them have a good time, and all I get is abuse, the existence of a hunted man."

That's Al Capone speaking. Yes, America's most notorious Public Enemy—the most sinister gang leader who ever shot up Chicago. Capone didn't condemn himself. He actually regarded himself as a public benefactor—an unappreciated and misunderstood public benefactor.

And so did Dutch Schultz before he crumpled up under gangster bullets in Newark. Dutch Schultz, one of New York's most notorious rats, said in a newspaper interview that he was a public benefactor. And he believed it.

I have had some interesting correspondence with Lewis Lawes, who was warden of New York's infamous Sing Sing prison for many years, on this subject, and he declared that "few of the criminals in Sing Sing regard themselves as bad men. They are just as human as you and I. So they rationalize, they explain. They can tell you why they had to crack a safe or be quick on the trigger finger. Most of them attempt by a form of reasoning, fallacious or logical, to justify their antisocial acts even to themselves, consequently stoutly maintaining that they should never have been imprisoned at all."

If Al Capone, "Two Gun" Crowley, Dutch Schultz and the desperate men and women behind prison walls don't blame themselves for anything—what about the people with whom you and I come in contact?

John Wanamaker, founder of the stores that bear his name, once confessed: "I learned thirty years ago that it is foolish to scold. I have enough trouble overcoming my own limitations without fretting over the fact that God has not seen fit to distribute evenly the gift of intelligence."

Wanamaker learned this lesson early, but I personally had to blunder through this old world for a third of a century before it even began to dawn upon me that ninety-nine times out of a hundred, people don't criticize themselves for anything, no matter how wrong it may be.

Criticism is futile because it puts a person on the defensive and usually makes him strive to justify himself. Criticism is dangerous, because it wounds a person's precious pride, hurts his sense of importance, and arouses resentment.

B. F. Skinner, the world-famous psychologist, proved through his experiments that an animal rewarded for good behavior will learn much more rapidly and retain what it learns far more effectively than an animal punished for bad behavior. Later studies have shown that the same applies to humans. By criticizing, we do not make lasting changes and often incur resentment.

Hans Selye, another great psychologist, said, "As much as we thirst for approval, we dread condemnation."

The resentment that criticism engenders can demoralize employees, family members, and friends, and still not correct the situation that has been condemned.

George B. Johnston of Enid, Oklahoma, is the safety coordinator for an engineering company. One of his responsibilities is to see that employees wear their hard hats whenever they are on the job in the field. He reported that whenever he came across workers who were not wearing hard hats, he would tell them with a lot of authority of the regulation and that they must comply. As a result he would get sullen acceptance, and often after he left, the workers would remove the hats.

He decided to try a different approach. The next time he found some of the workers not wearing their hard hats, he asked if the hats were uncomfortable or did not fit properly. Then he reminded the men in a pleasant tone of voice that the hat was designed to protect them from injury and suggested that it always be worn on the job. The result was increased compliance with the regulation with no resentment or emotional upset.

You will find examples of the futility of criticism bristling on a thousand pages of history. Take, for example, the famous quarrel between Theodore Roosevelt and President Taft—a quarrel that split the Republican party, put Woodrow Wilson in the White House, and wrote bold, luminous lines across the First World War and altered the flow of history. Let's review the facts quickly. When Theodore Roosevelt stepped out of the White House in 1908, he supported Taft, who was elected president. Then Theodore Roosevelt went off to Africa to shoot lions. When he returned, he exploded. He denounced Taft for his conservatism, tried to secure the nomination for a third term himself, formed the Bull Moose party, and all but demolished the GOP. In the election that followed, William Howard Taft and the Republican party carried only two states, Vermont and Utah—the most disastrous defeat the party had ever known.

Theodore Roosevelt blamed Taft, but did President Taft blame himself? Of course not. With tears in his eyes, Taft said: "I don't see how I could have done any differently from what I have."

Who was to blame? Roosevelt or Taft? Frankly, I don't know, and I don't care. The point I am trying to make is that all of Theodore Roosevelt's criticism didn't persuade Taft that he was wrong. It merely made Taft strive to justify himself and to reiterate with tears in his eyes: "I don't see how I could have done any differently from what I have."

Or, take the Teapot Dome oil scandal. It kept the newspapers ringing with indignation in the early 1920s. It rocked the nation! Within the memory of living men, nothing like it had ever happened before in American public life. Here are the bare facts of the scandal: Albert B. Fall, secretary of the interior in Harding's cabinet, was entrusted with the leasing of government oil reserves at Elk Hill and Teapot Dome—oil reserves that had been set aside for the future use of the Navy. Did Secretary Fall permit competitive bidding? No sir. He handed the fat, juicy contract outright to his friend Edward L. Doheny. And what did Doheny do? He gave Secretary Fall what he was pleased to call a "loan" of one hundred thousand dollars. Then. in a high-handed manner, Secretary Fall ordered United States Marines into the district to drive off competitors whose adjacent wells were sapping oil out of the Elk Hill reserves. These competitors, driven off their ground at the ends of guns and bayonets, rushed into court—and blew the lid off the Teapot Dome scandal. A stench arose so vile that it ruined the Harding administration, nauseated an entire nation, threatened to wreck the Republican party, and put Albert B. Fall behind prison bars.

Fall was condemned viciously—condemned as few men in public life have ever been. Did he repent? Never! Years later Herbert Hoover intimated in a public speech that President Harding's death had been due to mental anxiety and worry because a friend had betrayed him. When Mrs. Fall heard that, she sprang from her chair, she wept, she shook her fists at fate and screamed: "What? Harding betrayed by Fall? No! My husband never betrayed anyone. This whole house full of gold would not tempt my husband to do wrong. He is the one who has been betrayed and led to the slaughter and crucified."

There you are; human nature in action, wrongdoers, blaming everybody but themselves. We are all like that. So when you and I are tempted to criticize someone tomorrow, let's remember Al Capone, "Two Gun" Crowley, and Albert Fall. Let's realize that criticisms are like homing pigeons. They always return home. Let's realize that the person we are going to correct and condemn will probably justify himself or herself, and condemn us in return; or, like the gentle Taft, will say: "I don't see how I could have done any differently from what I have."

On the morning of April 15, 1865, Abraham Lincoln lay dying in a hall bedroom of a cheap lodging house directly across the street from Ford's Theater, where John Wilkes Booth had shot him. Lincoln's long body lay stretched diagonally across a sagging bed that was too short for him. A cheap reproduction of Rosa Bonheur's famous painting *The Horse Fair* hung above the bed, and a dismal gas jet flickered yellow light.

As Lincoln lay dying, Secretary of War Stanton said, "There lies the most perfect ruler of men that the world has ever seen."

What was the secret of Lincoln's success in dealing with people? I studied the life of Abraham Lincoln for ten years and devoted all of three years to writing and rewriting a book entitled *Lincoln the Unknown*. I believe I have made as detailed and exhaustive a study of Lincoln's personality and home life as it is possible for any being to make. I made a special study of Lincoln's method of dealing with people. Did he indulge in criticism? Oh, yes. As a young man in the Pigeon Creek Valley of Indiana, he not only criticized but also wrote letters and poems ridiculing people and dropped these letters on the country roads where they were sure to be found. One of these letters aroused resentments that burned for a lifetime.

Even after Lincoln had become a practicing lawyer in Springfield, Illinois, he attacked his opponents openly in letters published in the newspapers. But he did this just once too often.

In the autumn of 1842 he ridiculed a vain, pugnacious politician by the name of James Shields. Lincoln lampooned him through a anonymous letter published in the Springfield *Journal*. The town roared with laughter. Shields, sensitive and proud, boiled with indignation. He found out who wrote the letter, leaped on his horse, started after Lincoln, and challenged him to fight a duel. Lincoln didn't want to fight. He was opposed to dueling, but he couldn't get out of it and save his honor. He was given the choice of weapons. Since he had very long arms, he chose cavalry broadswords and took lessons in sword fighting from a West Point graduate. On the appointed day, he and Shields met on a sandbar in the Mississippi River, prepared to fight to the death, but at the last minute, their seconds interrupted and stopped the duel.

That was the most lurid personal incident in Lincoln's life. It taught him an invaluable lesson in the art of dealing with people. Never again did he write an insulting letter. Never again did he ridicule anyone. And from that time on, he almost never criticized anybody for anything.

Time after time, during the Civil War, Lincoln put a new general at the head of the Army of the Potomac, and each one in turn—McClellan, Pope, Burnside, Hooker, Meade—blundered tragically and drove Lincoln to pacing the floor in despair. Half the nation savagely condemned these incompetent generals, but Lincoln, "with malice toward none, with charity for all," held his peace. One of his favorite quotations was "Judge not, that ye be not judged."

And when Mrs. Lincoln and others spoke harshly of the southern people, Lincoln replied: "Don't criticize them; they are just what we would be under similar circumstances."

Yet if any man ever had occasion to criticize, surely it was Lincoln. Let's take just one illustration:

The Battle of Gettysburg was fought during the first three days of July 1863. During the night of July 4, Lee began to retreat southward while storm clouds deluged the country with rain. When Lee reached the Potomac with his defeated army, he found a swollen, impassible river in front of him, and a victorious Union Army behind him. Lee was in a trap. He couldn't escape. Lincoln saw that. Here was a golden, heaven-sent oppportunity—the opportunity to capture Lee's army and end the war immediately. So, with a surge of high hope, Lincoln ordered Meade not to call a council of war but to attack Lee immediately. Lincoln telegraphed his orders and then sent a special messenger to Meade demanding immediate action.

And what did General Meade do? He did the very opposite of what he was told to do. He called a council of war in direct violation of Lincoln's orders. He hesitated. He procrastinated. He telegraphed all manner of excuses. He refused point-blank to attack Lee. Finally the waters receded and Lee escaped over the Potomac with his forces.

Lincoln was furious. "What does this mean?" Lincoln cried to his son Robert. "Great God! What does this mean? We had them within our grasp, and had only to stretch forth our hands and they were ours; yet nothing I could say or do could make the army move. Under the circumstances, almost any general could have defeated Lee. If I had gone up there, I could have whipped him myself."

In bitter disappointment, Lincoln sat down and wrote Meade this letter. And remember, at this period of his life Lincoln was extremely conservative and restrained in his phraseology. So this letter coming from Lincoln in 1863 was tantamount to the severest rebuke.

My dear General,
    I do not believe you appreciate the magnitude of the misfortune involved in Lee's escape. He was within our easy grasp, and to have closed upon him would, in connection with our other late successes, have ended the war. As it is, the war will be prolonged indefinitely. If you could not safely attack Lee last Monday, how can you possibly do so south of the river, when you can take with you very few— no more than two-thirds of the force you then had in hand? It would be unreasonable to expect and I do not expect that you can now effect much. Your

golden opportunity is gone, and I am distressed immeasurably because of it.

What do you suppose Meade did when he read the letter?

Meade never saw that letter. Lincoln never mailed it. It was found among his papers after his death.

My guess is—and this is only a guess—that after writing that letter, Lincoln looked out of the window and said to himself, "Just a minute. Maybe I ought not to be so hasty. It is easy enough for me to sit here in the quiet of the White House and order Meade to attack; but if I had been up at Gettysburg, and if I had seen as much blood as Meade has seen during the last week, and if my ears had been pierced with the screams and shrieks of the wounded and dying, maybe I wouldn't be so anxious to attack either. If I had Meade's timid temperament, perhaps I would have done just what he had done. Anyhow, it is water under the bridge now. If I send this letter, it will relieve my feelings, but it will make Meade try to justify himself. It will make him condemn me. It will arouse hard feelings, impair all his further usefulness as a commander, and perhaps force him to resign from the army."

So, as I have already said, Lincoln put the letter aside, for he had learned by bitter experience that sharp criticisms and rebukes almost invariably end in futility.

Theodore Roosevelt said that when he, as president, was confronted with a perplexing problem, he used to lean back and look up at a large painting of Lincoln that hung above his desk in the White House and ask himself, "What would Lincoln do if he were in my shoes? How would he solve this problem?"

The next time we are tempted to admonish somebody, let's pull a five-dollar bill out of our pocket, look at Lincoln's picture on the bill, and ask, "How would Lincoln handle this problem if he had it?"

Mark Twain lost his temper occasionally and wrote letters that turned the paper brown. For example, he once wrote to a man who had aroused his ire: "The thing for you is a burial permit. You have only to speak and I will see that you get it." On another occasion he wrote to an editor about a proofreader's attempts to "improve my spelling and punctuation." He ordered: "Set the matter according to my copy hereafter and see that the proofreader retains his suggestions in the mush of his decayed brain."

The writing of these stinging letters made Mark Twain feel better. They allowed him to blow off steam, and the letters didn't do any real harm, because Mark's wife secretly lifted them out of the mail. They were never sent.

Do you know someone you would like to change and regulate and improve? Good! This is fine. I am all in favor of it. But why not begin on yourself? From a purely selfish standpoint, that is a lot more profitable than trying to improve others—yes, and a lot less dangerous. "Don't complain about the snow on your neighbor's roof," said Confucius, "when your own doorstep is unclean."

When I was still young and trying hard to impress people, I wrote a foolish letter to Richard Harding Davis, an author who once loomed large on the literary horizon of America. I was preparing a magazine article about authors, and I asked Davis to tell me about his method of work. A few weeks earlier, I had received a letter from someone with this notation at the bottom: "Dictated but not read." I was quite impressed. I felt that the writer must be very big and busy and important. I wasn't the slightest bit busy, but I was eager to make an impression on Richard Harding Davis, so I ended my short note with the words: "Dictated but not read."

He never troubled to answer the letter. He simply returned it to me with this scribbled across the bottom: "Your bad manners are exceeded only by your bad manners." True, I had blundered, and perhaps I deserved this rebuke. But, being human, I resented it. I resented it so sharply that when I read of the death of Richard Harding Davis ten years later, the one thought that still persisted in my mind—I am ashamed to admit—was the hurt he had given me.

If you and I want to stir up a resentment tomorrow that may rankle across the decades and endure until death, just let us indulge in a little stinging criticism.

When dealing with people, let us remember we are not dealing with creatures of logic. We are dealing with creatures of emotion, creatures bristling with prejudices and motivated by pride and vanity.

Bitter criticism caused the sensitive Thomas Hardy, one of the finest novelists ever to enrich English literature, to give up forever the writing of fiction. Criticism drove Thomas Chatterton, the English poet, to suicide.

Benjamin Franklin, tactless in his youth, became so diplomatic, so adroit at handling people, that he was made American ambassador to France. The secret of his success? "I will speak ill of no man," he said, ". . . and speak all the good I know of everybody."

Any fool can criticize, condemn, and complain—and most fools do.

But it takes character and self-control to be understanding and forgiving.

"A great man shows his greatness," said Carlyle, "by the way he treats little men."

Bob Hoover, a famous test pilot and frequent performer at air shows, was returning to his home in Los Angeles from an air show in San Diego. As described in the magazine *Flight Operations*, at three hundred feet in the air, both engines suddenly stopped. By deft maneuvering he managed to land the plane, but it was badly damaged although nobody was hurt.

Hoover's first act after the emergency landing was to

inspect the airplane's fuel. Just as he suspected, the World War II propeller plane he had been flying had been fueled with jet fuel rather than gasoline.

Upon returning to the airport, he asked to see the mechanic who had serviced his airplane. The young man was sick with the agony of his mistake. Tears streamed down his face as Hoover approached. He had just caused the loss of a very expensive plane and could have caused the loss of three lives as well.

You can imagine Hoover's anger. One could anticipate the tongue-lashing that this proud and precise pilot would unleash for that carelessness. But Hoover didn't scold the mechanic; he didn't even criticize him. Instead, he put his big arm around the man's shoulder and said, "To show you I'm sure that you'll never do this again, I want you to service my F-51 tomorrow."

Often parents are tempted to criticize their children. You would expect me to say "Don't." But I will not. I am merely going to say, "*Before* you criticize them, read one of the classics of American journalism, 'Father Forgets.' " It originally appeared as an editorial in the *People's Home Journal*. We are reprinting it here with the author's permission, as condensed in the *Reader's Digest*.

"Father Forgets" is one of those little pieces that— dashed off in a moment of sincere feeling—strikes an echoing chord in so many readers as to become a perennial reprint favorite. Since its first appearance, "Father Forgets" has been reproduced, writes the author, W. Livingston Larned, "in hundreds of magazines and house organs, and in newspapers the country over. It has been reprinted almost as extensively in many foreign languages. I have given personal permission to thousands who wished to read it from school, church, and lecture platforms. It has been 'on the air' on countless occasions and programs. Oddly enough, college periodicals have used it, and high-school magazines. Sometimes a little piece seems mysteriously to 'click.' This one certainly did."

FATHER FORGETS
W. Livingston Larned

Listen, son: I am saying this as you lie asleep, one little paw crumpled under your cheek and the blond curls stickily wet on your damp forehead. I have stolen into your room alone. Just a few minutes ago, as I sat reading my paper in the library, a stifling wave of remorse swept over me. Guiltily I came to your bedside.

There are the things I was thinking, son: I had been cross to you. I scolded you as you were dressing for school because you gave your face merely a dab with a towel. I took you to task for not cleaning your shoes. I called out angrily when you threw some of your things on the floor.

At breakfast I found fault, too. You spilled things. You gulped down your food. You put your elbows on the table. You spread butter too thick on your bread. And as you started off to play and I made for my train, you turned and waved a hand and called, "Goodbye, Daddy!" and I frowned, and said in reply, "Hold your shoulders back!"

Then it began all over again in the late afternoon. As I came up the road I spied you, down on your knees, playing marbles. There were holes in your stockings. I humiliated you before your boyfriends by marching you ahead of me to the house. Stockings were expensive—and if you had to buy them you would be more careful! Imagine that, son, from a father!

Do you remember, later, when I was reading in

the library, how you came in timidly, with a sort of hurt look in your eyes? When I glanced up over my paper, impatient at the interruption, you hesitated at the door. "What is it you want?" I snapped.

You said nothing, but ran across in one tempestuous plunge, and threw your arms around my neck and kissed me, and your small arms tightened with an affection that God had set blooming in your heart and which even neglect could not wither. And then you were gone, pattering up the stairs.

Well, son, it was shortly afterwards that my paper slipped from my hands and a terrible sickening fear came over me. What has habit been doing to me? The habit of finding fault, of reprimanding—this was my reward to you for being a boy. It was not that I did not love you; it was that I expected too much of youth. I was measuring you by the yardstick of my own years.

And there was so much that was good and fine and true in your character. The little heart of you was as big as the dawn itself over the wide hills. This was shown by your spontaneous impulse to rush in and kiss me good night. Nothing else matters tonight, son. I have come to your bedside in the darkness, and I have knelt there, ashamed!

It is a feeble atonement; I know you would not understand these things if I told them to you during your waking hours. But tomorrow I will be a real daddy! I will chum with you, and suffer when you suffer, and laugh when you laugh. I will bite my tongue when impatient words come. I will keep saying as if it were a ritual: "He is nothing but a boy—a little boy!"

I am afraid I have visualized you as a man. Yet as I see you now, son, crumpled and weary in your cot,

I see that you are still a baby. Yesterday you were in
your mother's arms, your head on her shoulder. I
have asked too much, too much.

Instead of condemning people, let's try to understand
them. Let's try to figure out why they do what they do.
That's a lot more profitable and intriguing than criticism;
and it breeds sympathy, tolerance, and kindness. "To know
all is to forgive all."

As Dr. Johnson said: "God himself, sir, does not pro-
pose to judge man until the end of his days."

Why should you and I?

Don't criticize, condemn, or complain.

9

The Big Secret of Dealing with People

There is only one way under high heaven to get anybody to do anything. Did you ever stop to think of that? Yes, just one way. And that is by making the other person want to do it.

Remember, there is no other way.

Of course, you can make someone want to give you his watch by sticking a revolver in his ribs. You can make your employees give you cooperation—until your back is turned—by threatening to fire them. You can make a child do what you want it to do by a whip or a threat. But these crude methods have sharply undesirable repercussions.

The only way I can get you to do anything is by giving you what you want.

What do you want?

Sigmund Freud said that everything you and I do springs from two motives: the sex urge and the desire to be great.

John Dewey, one of America's most profound philosophers, phrased it a bit differently. Dr. Dewey said that the

deepest urge in human nature is "the desire to be important." Remember that phrase: "the desire to be important."
It is significant. You are going to hear a lot about it in this
book.

What do you want? Not many things, but the few things
that you do wish, you crave with an insistence that will not
be denied. Some of the things most people want include:

1. Health and the preservation of life
2. Food
3. Sleep
4. Money and the things money will buy
5. Life in the hereafter
6. Sexual gratification
7. The well-being of our children
8. A feeling of importance

Almost all these wants are usually gratified—all except
one. But there is one longing—almost as deep, almost as
imperious, as the desire for food or sleep—that is seldom
gratified. It is what Freud calls "the desire to be great." It is
what Dewey calls "the desire to be important."

Lincoln once began a letter saying: "Everybody likes a
compliment." William James said: "The deepest principle
in human nature is the craving to be appreciated." He
didn't speak, mind you, of the "wish" or the "desire" or
the "longing" to be appreciated. He said the "craving" to
be appreciated.

Here is a gnawing and unfaltering human hunger, and
the rare individual who honestly satisfies this heart hunger
will hold people in the palm of his or her hand and "even
the undertaker will be sorry when he dies."

The desire for a feeling of importance is one of the chief
distinguishing differences between mankind and the animals. To illustrate: When I was a farm boy out in Missouri,

my father bred fine Duroc-Jersey hogs and pedigreed white-faced cattle. We used to exhibit our hogs and white-faced cattle at the country fairs and livestock shows throughout the Middle West. We won first prizes by the score. My father pinned his blue ribbons on a sheet of white muslin, and when friends or visitors came to the house, he would get out the long sheet of muslin. He would hold one end and I would hold the other while he exhibited the blue ribbons.

The hogs didn't care about the ribbons they had won. But Father did. These prizes gave him a feeling of importance.

If our ancestors hadn't had this flaming urge for a feeling of importance, civilization would have been impossible. Without it, we should have been just about like animals.

It was this desire for a feeling of importance that inspired Dickens to write his immortal novels. This desire inspired Sir Christopher Wren to design his symphonies in stone. This desire made Rockefeller amass millions that he never spent! And this same desire made the richest family in your town build a house far too large for its requirements.

This desire makes you want to wear the latest styles, drive the latest cars, and talk about your brilliant children.

It is this desire that lures many boys and girls into joining gangs and engaging in criminal activities. The average young criminal, according to E. P. Mulrooney, onetime police commissioner of New York, is filled with ego, and his first request after arrest is for those lurid newspapers that make him out a hero. The disagreeable prospect of serving time seems remote so long as he can gloat over his likeness sharing space with pictures of sports figures, movie and television stars, and politicians.

If you tell me how you get your feeling of importance, I'll tell you what you are. That determines your character. That is the most significant thing about you. For example,

John D. Rockefeller got his feeling of importance by giving money to erect a modern hospital in Peking, China, to care for millions of poor people whom he had never seen and never would see. Dillinger, on the other hand, got his feeling of importance by being a bandit, a bank robber and killer. When the FBI agents were hunting him, he dashed into a farmhouse up in Minnesota and said, "I'm Dillinger!" He was proud of the fact that he was Public Enemy Number One. "I'm not going to hurt you, but I'm Dillinger!" he said.

Yes, the one significant difference between Dillinger and Rockefeller is how they got their feeling of importance.

History sparkles with amusing examples of famous people struggling for a feeling of importance. Even George Washington wanted to be called "His Mightiness, the President of the United States"; and Columbus pleaded for the title "Admiral of the Ocean and Viceroy of India." Catherine the Great refused to open letters that were not addressed to "Her Imperial Majesty"; and Mrs. Lincoln, in the White House, turned upon Mrs. Grant like a tigress and shouted, "How dare you be seated in my presence until I invite you!"

Our millionaires helped finance Admiral Byrd's expedition to the Antarctic in 1928 with the understanding that ranges of icy mountains would be named after them; and Victor Hugo aspired to have nothing less than the city of Paris renamed in his honor. Even Shakespeare, mightiest of the mighty, tried to add luster to his name by procuring a coat of arms for his family.

People sometimes become invalids in order to win sympathy and attention, and get a feeling of importance. For example, take Mrs. McKinley. She got a feeling of importance by forcing her husband, the President of the United States, to neglect important affairs of state while he reclined on the bed beside her for hours at a time, his arm about her, soothing her to sleep. She fed her gnawing desire for attention by insisting that he remain with her while she was having her teeth fixed, and once created a stormy scene when he had to leave her alone with the dentist while he kept an appointment with John Hay, his secretary of state.

The writer Mary Roberts Rinehart once told me of a bright, vigorous young woman who became an invalid in order to get a feeling of importance. "One day," said Mrs. Rinehart, "this woman had been obliged to face something, her age perhaps. The lonely years were stretching ahead and there was little left for her to anticipate.

"She took to her bed; and for ten years her old mother traveled to the third floor and back, carrying trays, nursing her. Then one day the old mother, weary with service, lay down and died. For some weeks, the invalid languished; then she got up, put on her clothing, and resumed living again."

Some authorities declare that people may actually go insane in order to find, in the dreamland of insanity, the feeling of importance that has been denied them in the harsh world of reality. There are more patients suffering from mental diseases in the United States than from all other diseases combined.

What is the cause of insanity?

Nobody can answer such a sweeping question, but we know that certain diseases, such as syphilis, break down and destroy the brain cells and result in insanity. In fact, about one-half of all mental diseases can be attributed to such physical causes as brain lesions, alcohol, toxins, and injuries. But the other half—and this is the appalling part of the story—the other half of the people who go insane apparently have nothing organically wrong with their brain cells. In post-mortem examinations, when their brain tissues are studied under the highest-powered microscopes, these tissues are found to be apparently just as healthy as yours and mine.

Why do these people go insane?

I put that question to the head physician of one of our most important psychiatric hospitals. This doctor, who has received the highest honors and the most coveted awards for his knowledge of this subject, told me frankly that he didn't know why people went insane. Nobody knows for sure. But he did say that many people who go insane find in insanity a feeling of importance that they were unable to achieve in the world of reality. Then he told me this story:

"I have a patient right now whose marriage proved to be a tragedy. She wanted love, sexual gratification, children, and social prestige, but life blasted all her hopes. Her husband didn't love her. He refused even to eat with her and forced her to serve his meals in his room upstairs. She had no children, no social standing. She went insane; and, in her imagination, she divorced her husband and resumed her maiden name. She now believes she has married into English aristocracy, and she insists on being called Lady Smith.

"And as for children, she imagines now that she has had a new child every night. Each time I call on her she says: 'Doctor, I had a baby last night.' "

Life once wrecked all her dream ships on the sharp rocks of reality; but in the sunny, fantasy isles of insanity, all her barkentines race into port with canvas billowing and winds singing through the sails.

Tragic? Oh, I don't know. Her physician said to me: "If I could stretch out my hand and restore her sanity, I wouldn't do it. She's much happier as she is."

If some people are so hungry for a feeling of importance that they actually go insane to get it, imagine what miracle you and I can achieve by giving people honest appreciation this side of insanity.

One of the first people in American business to be paid a salary of over a million dollars a year (when there was no income tax and a person earning fifty dollars a week was considered well off) was Charles Schwab. He had been picked by Andrew Carnegie to become the first president of the newly formed United States Steel Company in 1921, when Schwab was only thirty-eight years old. (Schwab later left U.S. Steel to take over the then troubled Bethlehem Steel Company, and he rebuilt it into one of the most profitable companies in America.)

Why did Andrew Carnegie pay a million dollars a year, or more than three thousand dollars a day, to Charles Schwab? Why? Because Schwab was a genius? No. Because he knew more about the manufacture of steel than other people? Nonsense. Charles Schwab told me himself that he had many men working for him who knew more about the manufacture of steel than he did.

Schwab says that he was paid this salary largely because of his ability to deal with people. I asked him how he did it. Here is his secret set down in his own words—words that ought to be cast in eternal bronze and hung in every home and school, every shop and office in the land; words that children ought to memorize instead of wasting their time memorizing the conjugation of Latin verbs or the amount of the annual rainfall in Brazil; words that will all but transform your life and mine if we will only live them:

"I consider my ability to arouse enthusiasm among my people," said Schwab, "the greatest asset I possess, and the way to develop the best that is in a person is by appreciation and encouragement.

"There is nothing else that so kills the ambitions of a person as criticisms from superiors. I never criticize anyone. I believe in giving a person incentive to work. So I am anxious to praise but loath to fault. If I like anything, *I am hearty in my approbation and lavish in my praise.*"

That is what Schwab did. But what do average people do? The exact opposite. If they don't like a thing, they bawl out their subordinates; if they do like it, they say nothing. As the old couplet says: "Once I did bad and that I heard ever / Twice I did good, but that I heard never."

"In my wide association in life, meeting with many and great people in various parts of the world," Schwab declared, "I have yet to find the person, however great and exalted his station, who did not do better work and put forth greater effort under a spirit of approval than he would ever do under a spirit of criticism."

That, he said frankly, was one of the outstanding reasons for the phenomenal success of Andrew Carnegie. Carnegie praised his associates publicly as well as privately.

Carnegie wanted to praise his assistants even on his tombstone. He wrote an epitaph for himself that read: "Here lies one who knew how to get around him men who were cleverer than himself."

Sincere appreciation was one of the secrets of the first John D. Rockefeller's success in handling men. For example, when one of his partners, Edward T. Bedford, lost a million dollars for the firm by a bad buy in South America, John D. might have criticized; but he knew Bedford had done his best—and the incident was closed. So Rockefeller found something to praise; he congratulated Bedford because he had been able to save sixty percent of the money he had invested. "That's splendid," said Rockefeller. "We don't always do as well as that upstairs."

I have among my clippings a story that I know never happened, but it illustrates a truth, so I'll repeat it:

According to this silly story, a farm woman, at the end of a heavy day's work, set before her menfolks a heaping pile of hay. And when they indignantly demanded whether she had gone crazy, she replied: "Why, how did I know you'd notice? I've been cooking for you men for the last twenty years and in all that time I ain't heard no word to let me know you wasn't just eating hay."

When a study was made a few years ago on runaway wives, what do you think was discovered to be the main reasons wives ran away? It was "lack of appreciation." And I'd bet that a similar study made of runaway husbands would come out the same way. We often take our spouses so much for granted that we never let them know we appreciate them.

A member of one of our classes told of a request made by his wife. She and a group of other women in her church were involved in a self-improvement program. She asked her husband to help her by listing six things he believed she could do to help her become a better wife. He reported to the class: "I was surprised by such a request. Frankly, it would have been easy for me to list six things I would like to change about her—my heavens, she could have listed a thousand things she would like to change about me—but I didn't. I said to her, 'Let me think about it and give you an answer in the morning.'

"The next morning I got up very early and called the florist and had them send six red roses to my wife with a note saying: 'I can't think of six things I would like to change about you. I love you the way you are.'

"When I arrived at home that evening, who do you think greeted me at the door: That's right. My wife! She was almost in tears. Needless to say, I was extremely glad I had not criticized her as she had requested.

"The following Sunday at church, after she had reported the results of her assignment, several women with whom she had been studying came up to me and said, 'That was the most considerate thing I have ever heard.' It was then I realized the power of appreciation."

Florenz Ziegfeld, the most spectacular producer who

ever dazzled Broadway, gained his reputation by his subtle ability to "glorify the American girl." Time after time, he took drab litle creatures that no one ever looked at twice and transformed them on the stage into glamorous visions of mystery and seduction. Knowing the value of appreciation and confidence, he made women feel beautiful by the sheer power of his gallantry and consideration. He was practical: he raised the salary of chorus girls from $30 a week to as high as $175. And he was also chivalrous; on opening night at the Follies, he sent telegrams to the stars in the cast, and he deluged every chorus girl in the show with American Beauty roses.

I once succumbed to the fad of fasting and went for six days and nights without eating. It wasn't difficult. I was less hungry at the end of the sixth day than I was at the end of the second. Yet I know, as you know, people who would think they had committed a crime if they let their families or employees go for six days without food; but they will let them go for six days, and six weeks, and sometimes sixty years without giving them the hearty appreciation that they crave almost as much as they crave food.

When Alfred Lunt, one of the great actors of his time, played the leading role in *Reunion in Vienna*, he said, "There is nothing I need so much as nourishment for my self-esteem."

We nourish the bodies of our children and friends and employees, but how often do we nourish their self-esteem? We provide them with roast beef and potatoes to build energy, but we neglect to give them kind words of appreciation that would sing in their memories for years like the music of the morning stars.

Paul Harvey, in one of his radio broadcasts, "The Rest of the Story," told how showing sincere appreciation can change a person's life. He reported that years ago a teacher in Detroit asked Stevie Morris to help her find a mouse that was lost in the classroom. You see, she appreciated the fact that nature had given Stevie something no one else in the room had. Nature had given Stevie a remarkable pair of ears to compensate for his blind eyes. But this was really the first time Stevie had been shown appreciation for those talented ears. Now, years later, he says that this act of appreciation was the beginning of a new life. You see, from that time on he developed his gift of hearing and went on to become, under the stage name of Stevie Wonder, one of *the* great pop singers and songwriters of the seventies.*

Some readers are saying right now as they read these lines; "Oh, phooey! *Flattery! Bear oil!* I've tried that stuff. It doesn't work—not with intelligent people."

Of course, flattery seldom works with discerning people. It is shallow, selfish, and insincere. It ought to fail and it usually does. True, some people are so hungry, so thirsty, for appreciation that they will swallow anything, just as a starving man will eat grass and fishworms.

Even Queen Victoria was susceptible to flattery. Prime Minister Benjamin Disraeli confessed that he laid it on thick in dealing with the queen. To use his exact words, he said he "spread it on with a trowel." But Disraeli was one of the most polished, deft, and adroit men who ever ruled the far-flung British Empire. He was a genius in his line. What would work for him wouldn't necessarily work for you and me. In the long run, flattery will do you more harm than good. Flattery is counterfeit, and like counterfeit money, it will eventually get you into trouble if you pass it to someone else.

The difference between appreciation and flattery? That is simple. One is sincere and the other insincere. One comes from the heart out; the other from the teeth out. One

*Paul Aurandt, *Paul Harvey's The Rest of the Story* (New York: Doubleday, 1977). Edited and compiled by Lynne Harvey. Copyright © by Paulynne, Inc.

is unselfish; the other selfish. One is universally admired; the other universally condemned.

I recently saw a bust of the Mexican hero General Álvaro Obregón in the Chapultepec palace in Mexico City. Below the bust are carved these wise words from General Obregón's philosophy: "Don't be afraid of enemies who attack you. Be afraid of friends who flatter you."

No! No! No! I am not suggesting flattery? Far from it. I'm talking about a new way of life. Let me repeat. *I am talking about a new way of life.*

King George V had a set of six maxims displayed on the walls of his study at Buckingham Palace. One of these maxims said: "Teach me neither to proffer nor receive cheap praise." That's all flattery is—cheap praise. I once read a definition of flattery that may be worth repeating: "Flattery is telling the other person precisely what he thinks about himself."

"Use what language you will," said Ralph Waldo Emerson, "you can never say anything but what you are."

If all we had to do was flatter, everybody would catch on and we should all be experts in human relations.

When we are not engaged in thinking about some definite problem, we usually spend about ninety-five percent of our time thinking about ourselves. Now, if we stop thinking about ourselves for a while and begin to think of the other person's good points, we won't have to resort to flattery so cheap and false that it can be spotted almost before it is out of the mouth.

One of the most neglected virtues of our daily existence is appreciation. Somehow, we neglect to praise our son or daughter when he or she brings home a good report card, and we fail to encourage our children when they first succeed in baking a cake or building a birdhouse. Nothing pleases children more than this kind of parental interest and approval.

The next time you enjoy filet mignon at the club, send

word to the chef that it was excellently prepared, and when a tired salesperson shows you unusual courtesy, please mention it.

Every minister, lecturer, and public speaker knows the discouragement of pouring himself or herself out to an audience and not receiving a single ripple of appreciative comment. What applies to professionals applies doubly to workers in offices, shops, and factories, and to our families and friends. In our interpersonal relations we should never forget that all our associates are human beings and hunger for appreciation. It is the legal tender that all souls enjoy.

Try leaving a friendly trail of little sparks of gratitude on your daily trips. You will be surprised how they will set small flames of friendship that will be rose beacons on your next visit.

Pamela Dunham of New Fairfield, Connecticut, had among her responsibilities on her job the supervision of a janitor who was doing a very poor job. The other employees would jeer at him and litter the hallways to show him what a bad job he was doing. It was so bad, productive time was being lost in the shop.

Without success, Pam tried various ways to motivate this person. She noticed that occasionally he did a particularly good piece of work. She made a point to praise him for it in front of the other people. Each day the job he did all around got better, and pretty soon he started doing all his work efficiently. Now he does an excellent job and other people give him appreciation and recognition. Honest appreciation got results where criticism and ridicule failed.

Hurting people not only does not change them, it is never called for. There is an old saying that I have cut out and pasted on my mirror, where I cannot help but see it every day:

I shall pass this way but once; any good, therefore, that I can do or any kindness that I can show to any human being, let me do it now. Let me not defer nor neglect it, for I shall not pass this way again.

Emerson said: "Every man I meet is my superior in some way. In that, I learn of him."

If that was true of Emerson, isn't it likely to be a thousand times more true of you and me? Let's cease thinking of our accomplishments, our wants. Let's try to figure out the other person's good points. Then forget flattery. Give honest, sincere appreciation. Be "hearty in your approbation and lavish in your praise," and people will cherish your words and treasure them and repeat them over a lifetime—repeat them years after you have forgotten them.

Give honest and sincere appreciation.

"He Who Can Do This Has the Whole World with Him. He Who Cannot Walks a Lonely Way"

I often went fishing up in Maine during the summer. Personally I am very fond of strawberries and cream, but I have found that for some strange reason, fish prefer worms. So when I went fishing, I didn't think about what I wanted. I thought about what they wanted. I didn't bait the hook with strawberries and cream. Rather, I dangled a worm or a grasshopper in front of the fish and said: "Wouldn't you like to have that?"

Why not use the same common sense when fishing for people?

That is what Lloyd George, Great Britain's prime minister during World War I, did. When someone asked him how he managed to stay in power after the other wartime leaders—Wilson, Orlando, and Clemenceau—had been forgotten, he replied that if his staying on top might be attributed to any one thing, it would be to his having learned that it was necessary to bait the hook to suit the fish.

Why talk about what we want? That is childish. Absurd. Of course, you are interested in what you want. You are eternally interested in it. But no one else is. The rest of us are just like you: we are interested in what we want.

So the only way on earth to influence other people is to talk about what *they* want and show them how to get it.

Remember that tomorrow when you are trying to get somebody to do something. If, for example, you don't want your children to smoke, don't preach at them, and don't talk about what you want; but show them that cigarettes may keep them from making the basketball team or winning the hundred-yard dash.

This is a good thing to remember regardless of whether you are dealing with children or calves or chimpanzees. For example: One day Ralph Waldo Emerson and his son tried to get a calf into a barn. But they made the common mistake of thinking only of what they wanted. Emerson pushed and his son pulled. But the calf was doing just what they were doing: he was thinking only of what he wanted; so he stiffened his legs and stubbornly refused to leave the pasture. The Irish housemaid saw their predicament. She couldn't write essays and books; but, on this occasion at least, she had more horse sense, or calf sense, than Emerson had. She thought of what the calf wanted; so she put her maternal finger in the calf's mouth and let the calf suck her finger as she gently led him into the barn.

Every act you have performed since the day you were born was performed because you wanted something. How about the time you gave a large contribution to the Red Cross? Yes, that is no exception to the rule. You gave the Red Cross the donation because you wanted to lend a helping hand; you wanted to do a beautiful, unselfish, divine act. "Inasmuch as ye have done it unto the least of these my brethren, ye have done it unto me."

If you hadn't wanted that feeling more than you wanted your money, you would not have made the contribution. Of course, you might have made the contribution because you were ashamed to refuse or because a customer asked you to do it. But one thing is certain. You made the contribution because you wanted something.

Harry A. Overstreet in his illuminating book *Influencing Human Behavior* said: "Action springs out of what we fundamentally desire . . . and the best piece of advice which can be given to would-be persuaders, whether in business, in the home, in the school, in politics, is: First, arouse in the other person an eager want. He who can do this has the whole world with him. He who cannot walks a lonely way."

Andrew Carnegie, the poverty-stricken Scotch lad who started to work at two cents an hour and finally gave away $365 million, learned early in life that the only way to influence people is to talk in terms of what the other person wants. He attended school only four years; yet he learned how to handle people.

To illustrate: His sister-in-law was worried sick over her two boys. They were at Yale, and they were so busy with their own affairs that they neglected to write home and paid no attention whatever to their mother's frantic letters.

Then Carnegie offered to wager a hundred dollars that he could get an answer by return mail, without even asking for it. Someone called his bet; so he wrote his nephews a chatty letter, mentioning casually in a postscript that he was sending each one a five-dollar bill.

He neglected, however, to enclose the money.

Back came replies by return mail thanking "Dear Uncle Andrew" for his kind note and—you can finish the sentence yourself.

Another example of persuading comes from Stan Novak

of Cleveland, Ohio, a participant in our course. Stan came home from work one evening to find his youngest son, Tim, kicking and screaming on the living room floor. He was to start kindergarten the next day and was protesting that he would not go. Stan's normal reaction would have been to banish the child to his room and tell him he'd just better make up his mind to go. He had no choice. But tonight, recognizing that this would not really help Tim start kindergarten in the best frame of mind, Stan sat down and thought, "If I were Tim, why would I be excited about going to kindergarten?" He and his wife made a list of all the fun things Tim would do such as finger-painting, singing songs, making new friends. Then they put them into action. "We all started finger-painting on the kitchen table—my wife, Lil, my other son, Bob, and myself, all having fun. Soon Tim was peeping around the corner. Next he was begging to participate. 'Oh, no! You have to go to kindergarten first to learn how to finger-paint.' With all the enthusiasm I could muster I went through the list talking in terms he could understand—telling him all the fun he would have in kindergarten. The next morning, I thought I was the first one up. I went downstairs and found Tim sitting sound asleep in the living room chair. 'What are you doing here?' I asked. 'I'm waiting to go to kindergarten. I don't want to be late.' The enthusiasm of our entire family had aroused in Tim an eager want that no amount of discussion or threat could have possibly accomplished."

Tomorrow you may want to persuade somebody to do something. Before you speak, pause and ask yourself: "How can I make this person want to do it?"

That question will stop us from rushing into a situation heedlessly, with futile chatter about our desires.

At one time I rented the grand ballroom of a certain New York hotel for twenty nights in each season in order to hold a series of lectures.

At the beginning of one season, I was suddenly informed that I should have to pay almost three times as much rent as formerly. This news reached me after the tickets had been printed and distributed and all announcements had been made.

Naturally, I didn't want to pay the increase, but what was the use of talking to the hotel about what I wanted? They were interested only in what they wanted. So a couple of days later I went to see the manager.

"I was a bit shocked when I got your letter," I said, "but I don't blame you at all. If I had been in your position, I should probably have written a similar letter myself. Your duty as the manager of the hotel is to make all the profit possible. If you don't do that, you will be fired and you ought to be fired. Now, let's take a piece of paper and write down the advantages and the disadvantages that will accrue to you, if you insist on this increase in rent."

Then I took a letterhead and ran a line through the center and headed one column "Advantages" and the other column "Disadvantages."

I wrote down under the head "Advantages" these words: "Ballroom free." Then I went on to say: "You will have the advantages of having the ballroom free to rent for dances and conventions. That is a big advantage, for affairs like that will pay you much more than you can get for a series of lectures. If I tie your ballroom up for twenty nights during the course of the season, it is sure to mean a loss of some very profitable business to you.

"Now, let's consider the disadvantages. First, instead of increasing your income from me, you are going to decrease it. In fact, you are going to wipe it out because I cannot pay the rent you are asking. I shall be forced to hold these lectures at some other place.

"There's another disadvantage to you also. These lectures attract crowds of educated and cultured people to your hotel. That is good advertising for you, isn't it? In fact, if you spent five thousand dollars advertising in the newspapers, you couldn't bring as many people to look at your hotel as I can bring by these lectures. That is worth a lot to a hotel, isn't it?"

As I talked, I wrote these two "disadvantages" under the proper heading, and handed the sheet of paper to the manager, saying: "I wish you would carefully consider both the advantages and the disadvantages that are going to accrue to you and then give me your final decision."

I received a letter the next day, informing me that my rent would be increased only fifty percent instead of three hundred percent.

Mind you, I got this reduction without saying a word about what I wanted. I talked all the time about what the other person wanted and how he could get it.

Suppose I had done the human, natural thing; suppose I had stormed into his office and said, "What do you mean by raising my rent three hundred percent when you know the tickets have been printed and the announcements made? Three hundred percent! Ridiculous! Absurd! I won't pay it!"

What would have happened then? An argument would have begun to steam and boil and sputter—and you know how arguments end. Even if I had convinced him that he was wrong, his pride would have made it difficult for him to back down and give in.

Here is one of the best bits of advice ever given about the fine art of human relationships. "If there is any one secret of success," said Henry Ford, "it lies in the ability to get the other person's point of view and see things from that person's angle as well as from your own."

That is so good, I want to repeat it: *"If there is any one secret of success, it lies in the ability to get the other person's point of view and see things from that person's angle as well as from your own."*

That is so simple, so obvious, that anyone ought to see the truth of it at a glance; yet ninety percent of the people on this earth ignore it ninety percent of the time.

An example? Look at the letters that come across your desk tomorrow morning, and you will find that most of them violate this important canon of common sense. Take this one, a letter written by the head of the radio department of an advertising agency with offices scattered across the continent. This letter was sent to the managers of local radio stations throughout the country. (I have set down, in brackets, my reactions to each paragraph.)

Mr. John Blank,
Blankville,
Indiana
Dear Mr. Blank:
The ——— company desires to retain its position in advertising agency leadership in the radio field.

[Who cares what your company desires? I am worried about my own problems. The bank is foreclosing the mortgage on my house, the bugs are destroying the hollyhocks, the stock market tumbled yesterday. I missed the eight-fifteen this morning, I wasn't invited to the Joneses' dance last night, the doctor tells me I have high blood pressure and neuritis and dandruff. And then what happens? I come down to the office this morning worried, open my mail, and here is some little whippersnapper off in New York yapping about what his company wants. Bah! If he only realized what sort of impression his letter makes, he would get out of the advertising business and start manufacturing sheep dip.]

This agency's national advertising accounts were the bulwark of the network. Our subsequent clearances of station time have kept us at the top of agencies year after year.

[You are big and rich and right at the top, aren't you? So what? I don't give two whoops in Hades if you are as big as General Motors and General Electric and the General Staff of the U.S. Army all combined. If you had as much sense as a half-witted hummingbird, you would realize that I am interested in how big I am—not how big you are. All this talk about your enormous success makes me feel small and unimportant.]

We desire to service our accounts with the last word on radio station information.

[You desire! You desire. You unmitigated ass. I'm not interested in what you desire or what the President of the United States desires. Let me tell you once and for all that I am interested in what I desire—and you haven't said a word about that yet in this absurd letter of yours.]

Will you, therefore, put the ―――― company on your preferred list for weekly station information— every single detail that will be useful to an agency in intelligently booking time.

["Preferred list." You have your nerve! You make me feel insignificant by your big talk about your company—and then you ask me to put you on a "preferred" list, and you don't even say "please" when you ask it.]

A prompt acknowledgment of this letter, giving us your latest "doings," will be mutually helpful.

[You fool! You mail me a cheap form letter, a letter scattered far and wide like the autumn leaves, and you have the gall to ask me, when I am worried about the mortgage and the hollyhocks and my blood pressure, to sit down and dictate a personal note acknowledging your form letter—and you ask me to do it "promptly." What do you mean, "promptly"? Don't you know I am just as busy as you are—or, at least, I like to think I am. And while we are on the subject, who gave you the lordly right to order me around? . . . You say it will be "mutually helpful." At last, at last, you have begun to see my viewpoint. But you are vague about how it will be to my advantage.]

> *Very truly yours,*
> *John Doe*
> *Manager, Radio Department*

> *P.S. The enclosed reprint from the Blankville* Journal *will be of interest to you, and you may want to broadcast it over your station.*

[Finally, down here in the postscript, you mention something that may help me solve one of my problems. Why didn't you begin your letter with—but what's the use? Any advertising man who is guilty of perpetrating such drivel as you have sent me has something wrong with his medulla oblongata. You don't need a letter giving our latest doings. What you need is a quart of iodine in your thyroid gland.]

Now, if people who devote their lives to advertising and who pose as experts in the art of influencing people to buy—if they write a letter like that, what can we expect from the butcher and baker or the auto mechanic?

Here is another letter, written by the superintendent of a large freight terminal to a student of this course, Edward Vermylen. What effect did this letter have on the man to whom it was addressed? Read it and then I'll tell you.

A. Zerega's Sons, Inc.
28 Front Street
Brooklyn, N.Y. 11201
Attention: Mr. Edward Vermylen

Gentlemen:
The operations at our outbound-rail-receiving station are handicapped because a material percentage of the total business is delivered us in the late afternoon. This condition results in congestion, overtime on the part of our forces, delays to trucks, and in some cases delays to freight. On November 10, we received from your company a lot of 510 pieces, which reached here at 4:20 P.M.

We solicit your cooperation toward overcoming the undesirable effects arising from late receipt of freight. May we ask that, on days on which you ship the volume which was received on the above date, effort be made either to get the truck here earlier or to deliver us part of the freight during the morning?

The advantage that would accrue to you under such an arrangement would be that of more expeditious discharge of your trucks and the assurance that your business would go forward on the date of its receipt.

Very truly yours,
J—— B——, Supt.

After reading this letter, Mr. Vermylen, sales manager for A. Zerega's Sons, Inc., sent it to me with the following comment:

This letter had the reverse effect from that which was intended. The letter begins by describing the

Terminal's difficulties, in which we are not interested, generally speaking. Our cooperation is then requested without any thought as to whether it would inconvenience us, and then, finally, in the last paragraph, the fact is mentioned that if we do cooperate it will mean more expeditious discharge of our trucks with the assurance that our freight will go forward on the date of its receipt.

In other words, that in which we are most interested is mentioned last and the whole effect is one of raising a spirit of antagonism rather than of cooperation.

Let's see if we can't rewrite and improve this letter. Let's not waste any time talking about our problems. As Henry Ford admonishes, let's "get the other person's point of view and see things from his or her angle, as well as from our own."

Here is one way of revising the letter. It may not be the best way, but isn't it an improvement?

Mr. Edward Vermylen
c/o A. Zerega's Sons, Inc.
28 Front St.
Brooklyn, N.Y. 11201

Dear Mr. Vermylen:

Your company has been one of our good customers for fourteen years. Naturally, we are very grateful for your patronage and are eager to give you the speedy, efficient service you deserve. However, we regret to say that it isn't possible for us to do that when your trucks bring us a large shipment late in the afternoon, as they did on November 10. Why? Because many other customers make late-afternoon deliveries also. Naturally, that causes congestion. That means your trucks are held up unavoidably at the pier and sometimes even your freight is delayed.

That's bad, but it can be avoided. If you make your deliveries at the pier in the morning when possible, your trucks will be able to keep moving, your freight will get immediate attention, and our workers will get home early at night to enjoy a dinner of the delicious macaroni and noodles that you manufacture.

Regardless of when your shipments arrive, we shall always cheerfully do all in our power to serve you promptly.

You are busy. Please don't trouble to answer this note.

Very truly yours,
J—— B——, Supt.

Barbara Anderson, who worked in a bank in New York, desired to move to Phoenix, Arizona, because of the health of her son. Using the principles she had learned in our course, she wrote the following letter to twelve banks in Phoenix:

Dear Sir:
My ten years of bank experience should be of interest to a rapidly growing bank like yours.

In various capacities in bank operations with the Bankers Trust Company in New York, leading to my present assignment as branch manager, I have acquired skills in all phases of banking, including depositor relations, credits, loans, and administration.

I will be relocating to Phoenix in May and I am sure I can contribute to your growth and profit. I will

be in Phoenix the week of April 3 and would appreciate the opportunity to show you how I can help your
bank meet its goals.

Sincerely,
Barbara L. Anderson

Do you think Mrs. Anderson received any response
from that letter? Eleven of the twelve banks invited her to
be interviewed, and she had a choice of which bank's offer
to accept. Why? Mrs. Anderson did not state what *she*
wanted, but wrote in the letter how she could help them,
and focused on *their* wants, not her own.

Thousands of salespeople are pounding the pavements
today, tired, discouraged, and underpaid. Why? Because
they are always thinking only of what they want. They
don't realize that neither you nor I want to buy anything. If
we did, we would go out and buy it. But both of us are
eternally interested in solving our problems. And if salespeople can show us how their services or merchandise will
help us solve our problems, they won't need to sell us.
We'll buy. And customers like to feel that they are buying—
not being sold.

Yet many salespeople spend a lifetime in selling without
seeing things from the customer's angle. For example, for
many years I lived in Forest Hills, a little community of
private homes in the center of Greater New York. One day
as I was rushing to the station, I chanced to meet a real-
estate operator who had bought and sold property in that
area for many years. He knew Forest Hills well, so I
hurriedly asked him whether or not my stucco house was
built with metal lath or hollow tile. He said he didn't know
and told me what I already knew—that I could find out by
calling the Forest Hills Garden Association. The following
morning, I received a letter from him. Did he give me the
information I wanted? He could have gotten it in sixty

seconds by a telephone call. But he didn't. He told me again that I could get it by telephoning, and then asked me to let him handle my insurance.

He was not interested in helping me. He was interested only in helping himself.

J. Howard Lucas of Birmingham, Alabama, tells how two salespeople from the same company handled the same type of situation. He reported:

"Several years ago I was on the management team of a small company. Headquarted near us was the district office of a large insurance company. Their agents were assigned territories, and our company was assigned to two agents, who I shall refer to as Carl and John.

"One morning, Carl dropped by our office and casually mentioned that his company had just introduced a new life insurance policy for executives and thought we might be interested later on and he would get back to us when he had more information on it.

"The same day, John saw us on the sidewalk while returning from a coffee break, and he shouted: 'Hey, Luke, hold up, I have some great news for you fellows.' He hurried up and very excitedly told us about an executive life insurance policy his company had introduced that very day. (It was the same policy that Carl had casually mentioned.) He wanted us to have one of the first issued. He gave us a few important facts about the coverage and ended saying, 'The policy is so new, I'm going to have someone from the home office come out tomorrow and explain it. Now, in the meantime, let's get the applications signed and on the way so he can have more information to work with.' His enthusiasm aroused in us an eager want for this policy even though we still did not have details. When they were made available to us, they confirmed John's initial understanding of the policy, and he not only sold each of us a policy, but later doubled our coverage.

"Carl could have had those sales, but he made no effort to arouse in us any desire for the policies."

The world is full of people who are grabbing and self-seeking. So the rare individual who unselfishly tries to serve others has an enormous advantage. He has little competition. Owen D. Young, a noted lawyer and one of America's great business leaders, once said: "People who can put themselves in the place of other people, who can understand the workings of their minds, need never worry about what the future has in store for them."

If out of reading this book you get just one thing—an increased tendency to think always in terms of other people's point of view, and see things from their angle—if you get that one thing out of this book, it may easily prove to be one of the building blocks of your career.

Looking at the other person's point of view and arousing an eager want for something is not to be construed as manipulating that person to do something that is only for your benefit and his or her detriment. Each party should gain from the negotiation. In the letters to Mr. Vermylen, both the sender and the receiver of the correspondence gained by implementing what was suggested. Both the bank and Mrs. Anderson won by her letter in that the bank obtained a valuable employee and Mrs. Anderson a suitable job. And in the example of John's sale of insurance to Mr. Lucas, both gained through the transaction.

Another example in which everybody gains through this principle of arousing an eager want comes from Michael E. Whidden of Warwick, Rhode Island, who is a territory salesman for the Shell Oil Company. Mike wanted to become the number-one salesperson in his district, but one service station was holding back. It was run by an older man who could not be motivated to clean up his station. It was in such poor shape that sales were declining significantly.

The manager would not listen to any of Mike's pleas to upgrade the station. After many exhortations and heart-to-heart talks—all of which had no impact—Mike decided to invite the manager to visit the newest Shell station in his territory.

The manager was so impressed by the facilities at the new station that when Mike visited him the next time, his station was cleaned up and had recorded a sales increase. This enabled Mike to reach the number-one spot in his district. All his talking and discussion hadn't helped, but by arousing an eager want in the manager, by showing him the modern station, he had accomplished his goal, and both the manager and Mike benefited.

Most people go through college and learn to read Virgil and master the mysteries of calculus without ever discovering how their own minds function. For instance: I once gave a course in Effective Speaking for the young college graduates who were entering the employ of the Carrier Corporation, the large air-conditioner manufacturer. One of the participants wanted to persuade the others to play basketball in their free time, and this is about what he said: "I want you to come out and play basketball. I like to play basketball, but the last few times I've been to the gymnasium there haven't been enough people to get up a game. Two or three of us got to throwing the ball around the other night—and I got a black eye. I wish all of you would come down tomorrow night. I want to play basketball."

Did he talk about anything you want? You don't want to go to a gymnasium that no one else goes to, do you? You don't care about what he wants. You don't want to get a black eye.

Could he have shown you how to get the things you want by using the gymnasium? Surely. More pep. Keener edge to the appetite. Clearer brain. Fun. Games. Basketball.

To repeat Professor Overstreet's wise advice: *First,*

arouse in the other person an eager want. He who can do this has the whole world with him. He who cannot walks a lonely way.

One of the students in the training course was worried about his little boy. The child was underweight and refused to eat properly. They scolded and nagged. "Mother wants you to eat this and that." "Father wants you to grow up to be a big man."

Did the boy pay any attention to these pleas? Just about as much as you would pay to one fleck of sand on a sandy beach.

No one with a trace of horse sense would expect a child three years old to react to the viewpoint of a father thirty years old. Yet that was precisely what that father had expected. It was absurd. He finally saw that. So he said to himself: "What does that boy want? How can I tie up what I want to what he wants?"

It was easy for the father when he started thinking about it. His boy had a tricycle that he loved to ride up and down the sidewalk in front of the house in Brooklyn. A few doors down the street lived a bully—a bigger boy who would pull the little boy off his tricycle and ride it himself.

Naturally, the little boy would run screaming to his mother, and she would have to come out and take the bully off the tricycle and put her little boy on again. This happened almost every day.

What did the little boy want? It didn't take a Sherlock Holmes to answer that one. His pride, his anger, his desire for a feeling of importance—all the strongest emotions in his makeup—goaded him to get revenge, to smash the bully in the nose. And when his father explained that the boy would be able to wallop the daylights out of the bigger kid someday if he would only eat the things his mother wanted him to eat—when his father promised him that—there was no longer any problem of dietetics. That boy would have eaten spinach, sauerkraut, salt mackerel—anything in order to be big enough to whip the bully who had humiliated him so often.

After solving that problem, the parents tackled another: the boy had the unholy habit of wetting the bed.

He slept with his grandmother. In the morning, his grandmother would wake up and feel the sheet and say: "Look, Johnny, what you did again last night."

He would say: "No, I didn't do it. You did it."

Scolding, spanking, shaming him, reiterating that the parents didn't want him to do it—none of these things kept the bed dry. So the parents asked: "How can we make this boy want to stop wetting his bed?".

What were his wants? First, he wanted to wear pajamas like Daddy instead of wearing a nightgown like Grandmother. Grandmother was getting fed up with his nocturnal iniquities, so she gladly offered to buy him a pair of pajamas if he would reform. Second, he wanted a bed of his own. Grandma did object.

His mother took him to a department store in Brooklyn, winked at the salesgirl, and said: "Here is a little gentleman who would like to do some shopping."

The salesgirl made him feel important by saying: "Young man, what can I show you?"

He stood a couple of inches taller and said: "I want to buy a bed for myself."

When he was shown the one his mother wanted him to buy, she winked at the salesgirl and the boy was persuaded to buy it.

The bed was delivered the next day; and that night, when Father came home, the little boy ran to the door shouting: "Daddy! Daddy! Come upstairs and see my bed that I bought!"

The father, looking at the bed, obeyed Charles Schwab's injunction: he was "hearty in his approbation and lavish in his praise."

"You are not going to wet this bed, are you?" the father said.

"Oh, no, no! I am not going to wet this bed." The boy kept his promise, for his pride was involved. That was his bed. He and he alone had bought it. And he was wearing pajamas now like a little man. He wanted to act like a man. And he did.

Another father, K. T. Dutschmann, a telephone engineer, a student of the training course, couldn't get his three-year-old daughter to eat breakfast food. The usual scolding, pleading, coaxing methods had all ended in futility. So the parents asked themselves: "How can we make her want to do it?"

The little girl loved to imitate her mother, to feel big and grown up; so one morning they put her on a chair and let her make the breakfast food. At just the psychological moment, Father drifted into the kitchen while she was stirring the cereal and she said: "Oh, look, Daddy, I am making the cereal this morning."

She ate two helpings of the cereal without any coaxing, because she was interested in it. She had achieved a feeling of importance; she had found in making the cereal an avenue of self-expression.

William Winter once remarked that "self-expression is the dominant necessity of human nature." Why can't we adapt this same psychology to business dealings? When we have a brilliant idea, instead of making others think it is ours, why not let them cook and stir the idea themselves? They will then regard it as their own; they will like it and maybe eat a couple of helpings of it.

Remember: "First, arouse in the other person an eager want. He who can do this has the whole world with him. He who cannot walks a lonely way."

Arouse in the other person an eager want.

11

Do This and You'll Be Welcome Anywhere

Why read this book to find out how to win friends? Why not study the technique of the greatest winner of friends the world has ever known? Who is he? You may meet him tomorrow coming down the street. When you get within ten feet of him, he will begin to wag his tail. If you stop and pat him, he will almost jump out of his skin to show you how much he likes you. And you know that behind this show of affection on his part, there are no ulterior motives: he doesn't want to sell you any real estate, and he doesn't want to marry you.

Did you ever stop to think that a dog is the only animal that doesn't have to work for a living? A hen has to lay eggs, a cow has to give milk, and a canary has to sing. But a dog makes his living by giving you nothing but love.

When I was five years old, my father bought a little yellow-haired pup for fifty cents. He was the light and joy of my childhood. Every afternoon about four-thirty, he would sit in the front yard with his beautiful eyes staring steadfastly at the path, and as soon as he heard my voice or saw me swinging my dinner pail through the buck brush, he was off like a shot, racing breathlessly up the hill to greet me with leaps of joy and barks of sheer ecstasy.

Tippy was my constant companion for five years. Then one tragic night—I shall never forget it—he was killed within ten feet of me, killed by lightning. Tippy's death was the tragedy of my boyhood.

You never read a book on psychology, Tippy. You didn't need to. You knew by some divine instinct that you can made more friends in two months by becoming genuinely interested in other people than you can in two years by trying to get other people interested in you. Let me repeat that. You can make more friends in two months by becoming interested in other people than you can in two years by trying to get other people interested in you.

Yet I know and you know people who blunder through life trying to wigwag other people into becoming interested in them.

Of course, it doesn't work. People are not interested in you. They are not interested in me. They are interested in themselves—morning, noon, and after dinner.

The New York Telephone Company made a detailed study of telephone conversations to find out which word is the most frequently used. You have guessed it: it is the personal prounoun "I." "I." "I." It was used 3,900 times in 500 telephone conversations. "I." "I." "I." "I."

When you see a group photograph that you are in, whose picture do you look for first?

If we merely try to impress people and get people interested in us, we will never have many true, sincere friends. Friends, real friends, are not made that way.

Napoleon tried it, and in his last meeting with Josephine he said: "Josephine, I have been as fortunate as any man ever was on this earth; and yet, at this hour, you are the only person in the world on whom I can rely." And historians doubt that he could rely even on her.

Alfred Adler, the famous Viennese psychologist, wrote a book entitled *What Life Should Mean to You.* In that book he says: "It is the individual who is not interested in his fellow men who has the greatest difficulties in life and provides the greatest injury to others. It is from among such individuals that all human failures spring."

You may read scores of erudite tomes on psychology without coming across a statement more significant for you and for me. Adler's statement is so rich with meaning that I am going to repeat it in italics:

> *It is the individual who is not interested in his fellow men who has the greatest difficulties in life and provides the greatest injury to others. It is from among such individuals that all human failures spring.*

I once took a course in short-story writing at New York University, and during that course the editor of a leading magazine talked to our class. He said he could pick up any one of the dozens of stories that drifted across his desk every day and after reading a few paragraphs he could feel whether or not the author liked people. "If the author doesn't like people," he said, "people won't like his or her stories."

This hard-boiled editor stopped twice in the course of his talk on fiction writing and apologized for preaching a sermon. "I am telling you," he said, "the same things your preacher would tell you, but remember, you have to be interested in people if you want to be a successful writer of stories."

If that is true of writing fiction, you can be sure it is true of dealing with people face-to-face.

I spent an evening in the dressing room of Howard Thurston the last time he appeared on Broadway—Thurston was the acknowledged dean of magicians. For forty years he had traveled all over the world, time and again, creating illusions, mystifying audiences, and making people gasp with astonishment. More than 60 million people had paid admission to his show, and he had made almost $2 million in profit.

I asked Mr. Thurston to tell me the secret of his success. His schooling certainly had nothing to do with it, for he ran away from home as a small boy, became a hobo, rode in boxcars, slept in haystacks, begged his food from door to door, and learned to read by looking out of boxcars at signs along the railway.

Did he have a superior knowledge of magic? No, he told me hundreds of books had been written about legerdemain and scores of people knew as much about it as he did. But he had two things that the others didn't have. First, he had the ability to put his personality across the footlights. He was a master showman. He knew human nature. Everything he did, every gesture, every intonation of his voice, every lifting of an eyebrow had been carefully rehearsed, and his actions were timed to split seconds. But, in addition to that, Thurston had a genuine interest in people. He told me that many magicians would look at the audience and say to themselves, "Well, there is a bunch of suckers out there, a bunch of hicks; I'll fool them all right." But Thurston's method was totally different. He told me that every time he went on stage he said to himself: "I am grateful because these people came to see me. They make it possible for me to make my living in a very agreeable way. I'm going to give them the very best I possibly can."

He declared he never stepped in front of the footlights without first saying to himself over and over: "I love my audience. I love my audience." Ridiculous? Absurd? You are privileged to think anything you like. I am merely passing it on to you without comment as a recipe used by one of the most famous magicians of all time.

George Dyke of North Warren, Pennsylvania, was

forced to retire from his service station business after thirty years when a new highway was constructed over the site of his station. It wasn't long before the idle days of retirement began to bore him, so he started filling in his time trying to play music on his old fiddle. Soon he was traveling the area to listen to music and talk with many of the accomplished fiddlers. In his humble and friendly way he became generally interested in learning the background and interests of every musician he met. Although he was not a great fiddler himself, he made many friends in this pursuit. He attended competitions and soon became known to the country music fans in the eastern part of the United States as "Uncle George, the Fiddle Scraper from Kinzua County." When we heard Uncle George, he was seventy-two and enjoying every minute of his life. By having a sustained interest in other people, he created a new life for himself at a time when most people consider their productive years over.

That, too, was one of the secrets of Theodore Roosevelt's astonishing popularity. Even his servants loved him. His valet, James E. Amos, wrote a book about him entitled *Theodore Roosevelt, Hero to His Valet*. In that book Amos relates this illuminating incident:

My wife one time asked the President about a bobwhite. She had never seen one and he described it to her fully. Sometime later, the telephone at our cottage rang. [Amos and his wife lived in a little cottage on the Roosevelt estate at Oyster Bay.] My wife answered it and it was Mr. Roosevelt himself. He had called her, he said, to tell her that there was a bobwhite outside her window and that if she would look out she might see it. Little things like that were so characteristic of him. Whenever he went by our cottage, even though we were out of sight, we would hear him call out: "Oo-oo-oo, Annie?" or "Oo-oo-

oo, James!" It was just a friendly greeting as he went by.

How could employees keep from liking a man like that? How could anyone keep from liking him?

Roosevelt called at the White House one day when the President and Mrs. Taft were away. His honest liking for humble people was shown by the fact that he greeted all the old White House servants by name, even the scullery maids.

"When he saw Alice, the kitchen maid," writes Archie Butt, "he asked her if she still made corn bread. Alice told him that she sometimes made it for the servants, but no one ate it upstairs.

" 'They show bad taste,' Roosevelt boomed, 'and I'll tell the President so when I see him.'

"Alice brought a piece to him on a plate, and he went over to the office eating it as he went and greeting gardeners and laborers as he passed. . . .

"He addressed each person just as he had addressed them in the past. Ike Hoover, who had been head usher at the White House for forty years, said with tears in his eyes, 'It is the only happy day we had in nearly two years, and not one of us would exchange it for a hundred-dollar bill.' "

The same concern for the seemingly unimportant people helped sales representative Edward M. Sykes, Jr., of Chatham, New Jersey, retain an account. "Many years ago," he reported, "I called on customers for Johnson and Johnson in the Massachusetts area. One account was a drug store in Hingham. Whenever I went into this store I would always talk to the soda clerk and sales clerk for a few minutes before talking to the owner to obtain his order. One day I went up to the owner of the store, and he told me to leave as he was not interested in buying J&J products anymore because he felt they were concentrating their activities on food and discount stores to the detriment of the small drugstore. I left with my tail between my legs and drove around the town for several hours. Finally, I decided to go back and try at least to explain our position to the owner of the store.

"When I returned I walked in and as usual said hello to the soda clerk and sales clerk. When I walked up to the owner, he smiled at me and welcomed me back. He then gave me double the usual order. I looked at him with surprise and asked him what had happened since my visit only a few hours earlier. He pointed to the young man at the soda fountain and said that after I had left, the boy had come over and said that I was one of the few salespeople who called on the store who even bothered to say hello to him and to the others in the store. He told the owner that if any salesperson deserved his business, it was I. The owner agreed and remained a loyal customer. I never forgot that to be genuinely interested in other people is a most important quality for a salesperson to possess—for any person, for that matter."

I have discovered from personal experience that one can win the attention and time and cooperation of even the most sought-after people by becoming genuinely interested in them. Let me illustrate.

Years ago I conducted a course in fiction writing at the Brooklyn Institute of Arts and Sciences, and we wanted such distinguished and busy authors as Kathleen Norris, Fannie Hurst, Ida Tarbell, Albert Payson Terhune, and Rupert Hughes to come to Brooklyn and give us the benefit of their experience. So we wrote them, saying we admired their work and were deeply interested in getting their advice and learning the secrets of their success.

Each of these letters was signed by about 150 students. We said we realized that these authors were busy—too busy to prepare a lecture. So we enclosed a list of questions for them to answer about themselves and their methods of work. They liked that. Who wouldn't like it? So they left their homes and traveled to Brooklyn to give us a helping hand.

By using the same method, I persuaded Leslie M. Shaw, secretary of the treasury in Theodore Roosevelt's cabinet; George W. Wickersham, attorney general in Taft's cabinet; William Jennings Bryan; Franklin D. Roosevelt; and many other prominent men to come to talk to the students of my courses in public speaking.

All of us, be we workers in a factory, clerks in an office, or even a king upon his throne—all of us like people who admire us. Take the German kaiser, for example. At the close of World War I he was probably the most savagely and universally despised man on this earth. Even his own nation turned against him when he fled over into Holland to save his neck. The hatred against him was so intense that millions of people would have loved to tear him limb from limb or burn him at the stake. In the midst of all this forest fire of fury, one little boy wrote the kaiser a simple, sincere letter glowing with kindliness and admiration. This little boy said that no matter what the others thought, he would always love Wilhelm as his emperor. The kaiser was deeply touched by his letter and invited the little boy to come see him. The boy came, so did his mother—and the kaiser married her. That little boy didn't need to read a book on how to win friends and influence people. He knew how instinctively.

If we want to make friends, let's put ourselves out to do things for other people—things that require time, energy, unselfishness, and thoughtfulness. When the Duke of Windsor was Prince of Wales, he was scheduled to tour South America, and before he started out on that tour he spent months studying Spanish so that he could make public talks in the language of the country; and the South Americans loved him for it.

For years I made it a point to find out the birthdays of my friends. How? Although I haven't the foggiest bit of faith in astrology, I began by asking the other party whether he believed the date of one's birth has anything to do with character and disposition. I then asked him or her to tell me the month and day of birth. If he or she said November 24, for example, I kept repeating to myself, "November 24, November 24." The minute my friend's back was turned, I wrote down the name and birthday and later would transfer it to a birthday book. At the beginning of each year, I had these birthday dates scheduled in my calendar pad so that they came to my attention automatically. When the natal day arrived, there was my letter or telegram. What a hit it made! I was frequently the only person on earth who remembered.

If we want to make friends, let's greet people with animation and enthusiasm. When somebody calls you on the telephone use the same psychology. Say "Hello" in tones that bespeak how pleased you are to have the person call. Many companies train their telephone operators to greet all callers in a tone that radiates interest and enthusiasm. The callers feel the company is concerned about them. Let's remember that when we answer the telephone tomorrow.

Showing a genuine interest in others not only wins friends for you, but may develop in its customers a loyalty to your company. In an issue of the publication of the National Bank of North America of New York, the followng letter from Madeline Rosedale, a depositor, was published:

"I would like you to know how much I appreciate your staff. Everyone is so courteous, polite, and helpful. What a pleasure it is, after waiting on a long line, to have the teller greet you pleasantly.

"Last year my mother was hospitalized for five months. Frequently I went to Marie Petrucello, a teller. She was concerned about my mother and inquired about her progress."*

Is there any doubt that Mrs. Rosedale will continue to use this bank?

Charles R. Walters, of one of the large banks in New York City, was assigned to prepare a confidential report on a certain corporation. He knew of only one person who possessed the facts he needed so urgently. As Mr. Walters was ushered into the president's office, a young woman stuck her head through a door and told the president that she didn't have any stamps for him that day.

"I am collecting stamps for my twelve-year-old son," the president explained to Mr. Walters.

Mr. Walters stated his mission and began asking questions. The president was vague, general, nebulous. He didn't want to talk, and apparently nothing could persuade him to talk. The interview was brief and barren.

"Frankly, I didn't know what to do," Mr. Walters said as he related the story to the class. "Then I remembered what his secretary had said to him—stamps, twelve-year-old son. . . . And I also recalled that the foreign department of our bank collected stamps—stamps taken from letters pouring in from every continent washed by the seven seas.

"The next afternoon I called on this man and sent in word that I had some stamps for his boy. Was I ushered in with enthusiasm? Yes sir. He couldn't have shaken my hand with more enthusiasm if he had been running for Congress. He radiated smiles and good will. 'My George will love this one,' he kept saying as he fondled the stamps. 'And look at this! This is a treasure.'

"We spent half an hour talking stamps and looking at a picture of his boy, and he then devoted more than an hour of his time to giving me every bit of information I wanted—

*Eagle, publication of the National Bank of North America, New York, March 31, 1978.

without my even suggesting that he do it. He told me all he knew, and then called in his subordinates and questioned them. He telephoned some of his associates. He loaded me down with facts, figures, reports, and correspondence. In the parlance of newspaper reporters, I had a scoop."

Here is another illustration:

C. M. Knaphle, Jr., of Philadelphia, had tried for years to sell fuel to a large chain-store organization. But the chain-store company continued to purchase its fuel from an out-of-town dealer and haul it right past the door of Knaphle's office. Mr. Knaphle made a speech one night before one of my classes, pouring out his hot wrath upon chain stores, branding them as a curse on the nation.

And still he wondered why he couldn't sell them.

I suggested that he try different tactics. To put it briefly, this is what happened. We staged a debate between members of the course on whether the spread of the chain store is doing the country more harm than good.

Knaphle, at my suggestion, took the negative side; he agreed to defend the chain stores, and then went straight to an executive of the chain-store organization that he despised and said: "I am not here to try to sell fuel. I have come to ask you to do me a favor." He then told about his debate and said, "I have come to you for help because I can't think of anyone else who would be more capable of giving me the facts I want. I'm anxious to win this debate, and I'll deeply appreciate whatever help you can give me."

Here is the rest of the story in Mr. Knaphle's own words:

"I had asked this man for precisely one minute of his time. It was with this understanding that he consented to see me. After I had stated my case, he motioned me to a chair and talked to me for exactly one hour and forty-seven minutes. He called in another executive who had written a book about chain stores. He wrote to the National Chain

Store Association and secured for me a copy of a debate on the subject. He feels that the chain store is rendering a real service to humanity. He is proud of what he is doing for hundreds of communities. His eyes fairly glowed as he talked, and I must confess that he opened my eyes to things I had never dreamed of. He changed my whole mental attitude.

"As I was leaving, he walked with me to the door, put his arm around my shoulder, wished me well in my debate, and asked me to stop in and see him again and let him know how I made out. The last words he said to me were: 'Please see me again later in the spring. I should like to place an order with you for fuel.'

"To me that was almost a miracle. Here he was offering to buy fuel without my even suggesting it. I had made more headway in two hours by becoming genuinely interested in him and his problems than I could have made in ten years trying to get him interested in me and my product."

You didn't discover a new truth, Mr. Knaphle, for a long time ago, a hundred years before Christ was born, a Roman poet, Publilius Syrus, remarked: "We are interested in others when they are interested in us."

A show of interest, as with every other principle of human relations, must be sincere. It must pay off not only for the person showing the interest, but for the person receiving the attention. It is a two-way street—both parties benefit.

Martin Ginsberg, who took our course in Long Island, New York, reported how the special interest a nurse took in him profoundly affected his life:

"It was Thanksgiving Day and I was ten years old. I was in a welfare ward of a city hospital and was scheduled to undergo major orthopedic surgery the next day. I knew that I could only look forward to months of confinement, convalescence, and pain. My father was dead; my mother and I lived alone in a small apartment and we were on welfare. My mother was unable to visit me that day.

"As the day went on, I became overwhelmed with the feeling of loneliness, despair, and fear. I knew my mother was home alone worrying about me, not having anyone to be with, not having anyone to eat with, and not even having enough money to afford a Thanksgiving Day dinner.

"The tears welled up in my eyes, and I stuck my head under the pillow and pulled the covers over it. I cried silently, but oh so bitterly, so much that my body racked with pain.

"A young student nurse heard my sobbing and came over to me. She took the covers off my face and started wiping my tears. She told me how lonely she was, having to work that day and not being able to be with her family. She asked me whether I would have dinner with her. She brought two trays of food: sliced turkey, mashed potatoes, cranberry sauce, and ice cream for dessert. She talked to me and tried to calm my fears. Even though she was scheduled to go off duty at 4:00 P.M., she stayed on her own time until almost 11:00 P.M. She played games with me, talked to me, and stayed with me until I finally fell asleep.

"Many Thanksgivings have come and gone since I was ten, but one never passes without my remembering that particular one and my feelings of frustration, fear, loneliness, and the warmth and tenderness of the stranger who somehow made it all bearable."

If you want others to like you, if you want to develop real friendships, if you want to help others at the same time as you help yourself, keep this principle in mind:

Become genuinely interested in other people!

12

How to Make People Like You Instantly

I was waiting in line to register a letter in the post office at Thirty-third Street and Eighth Avenue in New York. I noticed that the clerk appeared to be bored with the job—weighing envelopes, handing out stamps, making change, issuing receipts—the same monotonous grind year after year. So I said to myself: "I am going to try to make that clerk like me. Obviously, to make him like me, I must say something nice, not about myself, but about him." So I asked myself, "What is there about him that I can honestly admire?" That is sometimes a hard question to answer, especially with strangers; but, in this case, it happened to be easy. I instantly saw something I admired no end.

So while he was weighing my envelope, I remarked with enthusiasm: "I certainly wish I had your head of hair."

He looked up, half-startled, his face beaming with smiles. "Well, it isn't as good as it used to be," he said modestly. I assured him that although it might have lost some of its pristine glory, nevertheless it was still magnificent. He was immensely pleased. We carried on a pleasant little conversation and the last thing he said to me was: "Many people have admired my hair."

I'll bet that person went out to lunch that day walking on air. I'll bet he went home that night and told his wife about it. I'll bet he looked in the mirror and said: "It is a beautiful head of hair."

I told this story once in public and a man asked me afterward: "What did you want to get out of him?"

What did I want to get out of him!!! What did I want to get out of him!!!

If we are so contemptibly selfish that we can't radiate a little happiness and pass on a bit of honest appreciation without trying to get something out of the other person in return—if our souls are no bigger than sour crab apples, we shall meet with the failure we so richly deserve.

Oh, yes, I did want something out of that chap. I wanted something priceless. And I got it. I got the feeling that I had done something for him without his being able to do anything whatever in return for me. That is a feeling that flows and sings in your memory long after the incident is past.

There is one all-important law of human conduct. If we obey that law, we shall almost never get into trouble. In fact, that law, if obeyed, will bring us countless friends and constant happiness. But the very instant we break the law, we shall get into endless trouble. The law is this: *Always make the other person feel important.* John Dewey, as we have already noted, said that the desire to be important is the deepest urge in human nature; and William James said: "The deepest principle in human nature is the craving to be appreciated." As I have already pointed out, it is this urge that differentiates us from the animals. It is this urge that has been responsible for civilization itself.

Philosophers have been speculating on the rules of human relationships for thousands of years, and out of all that speculation, there has evolved only one important precept. It is not new. It is as old as history. Zoroaster taught it to his followers in Persia twenty-five hundred years ago. Confucius preached it in China twenty-four centuries ago. Lao-tse, the founder of Taoism, taught it to his disciples in the Valley of the Han twenty-five centuries ago. Buddha preached it on the bank of the Holy Ganges five hundred years before Christ. The sacred books of Hinduism taught it a thousand years before that. Jesus taught it among the stony hills of Judea nineteen centuries ago. Jesus summed it up in one thought—probably the most important rule in the world: "Do unto others as you would have others do unto you."

You want the approval of those with whom you come in contact. You want recognition of your true worth. You want a feeling that you are important in your little world. You don't want to listen to cheap, insincere flattery, but you do crave sincere appreciation. You want your friends and associates to be, as Charles Schwab put it, "hearty in their approbation and lavish in their praise." All of us want that.

So let's obey the Golden Rule, and give unto others what we would have others give unto us.

How? When? Where? The answer is: All the time, everywhere.

David G. Smith of Eau Claire, Wisconsin, told one of our classes how he handled a delicate situation when he was asked to take charge of the refreshment booth at a charity concert.

"The night of the concert I arrived at the park and found two elderly ladies in a very bad humor standing next to the refreshment stand. Apparently each thought that she was in charge of this project. As I stood there pondering what to do, one of the members of the sponsoring committee appeared and handed me a cash box and thanked me for taking over the project. She introduced Rose and Jane as my helpers and then ran off.

"A great silence ensued. Realizing that the cash box

was a symbol of authority (of sorts), I gave the box to Rose and explained that I might not be able to keep the money straight and that if she took care of it I would feel better. I then suggested to Jane that she show two teenagers who had been assigned to refreshments how to operate the soda machine, and I asked her to be responsible for that part of the project.

"The evening was very enjoyable, with Rose happily counting the money, Jane supervising the teenagers, and me enjoying the concert."

You don't have to wait until you are ambassador to France or chairman of the Clambake Committee of your lodge before you use this philosophy of appreciation. You can work magic with it almost every day.

If, for example, the waitress brings us mashed potatoes when we have ordered French fried, let's say: "I'm sorry to trouble you, but I prefer French fried." She'll probably reply, "No trouble at all" and will be glad to change the potatoes, because we have shown respect for her.

Little phrases such as "I'm sorry to trouble you," "Would you be so kind as to?" "Won't you please?" "Would you mind?" "Thank you"—little courtesies like these relieve the monotonous grind of everyday life—and, incidentally, they are the hallmark of good breeding.

Let's take another illustration. Hall Caine's novels—*The Christian, The Deemster, The Manxman,* among others—were all best-sellers in the early part of this century. Millions of people read his novels, countless millions. He was the son of a blacksmith. He never had more than eight years' schooling in his life; yet when he died he was the richest literary man of his time.

The story goes like this: Hall Caine loved sonnets and ballads, so he devoured all of Dante Gabriel Rossetti's poetry. He even wrote an essay chanting the praises of Rossetti's artistic achievement—and sent a copy to Rossetti himself. Rossetti was delighted. "Any young man who has such an exalted opinion of my ability," Rossetti probably said to himself, "must be brilliant." So Rossetti invited this blacksmith's son to come to London and act as his secretary. That was the turning point in Hall Caine's life; for, in his new position, he met the literary artists of the day. Profiting by their advice and inspired by their encouragement, he launched upon a career that emblazoned his name across the sky.

His home, Greeba Castle, on the Isle of Man, became a Mecca for tourists from the far corners of the world, and he left a multimillion-dollar estate. Yet—who knows—he might have died poor and unknown had he not written an essay expressing his admiration for a famous man.

Such is the power, the stupendous power, of sincere, heartfelt appreciation.

Rossetti considered himself important. That is not strange. Almost everyone considers himself important, very important.

The life of many a person could probably be changed if only someone would make him feel important. Ronald J. Rowland, who is one of the instructors of our course in California, is also a teacher of arts and crafts. He wrote to us about a student named Chris in his beginning crafts class:

"Chris was a very quiet, shy boy lacking in self-confidence, the kind of student who often does not receive the attention he deserves. I also teach an advanced class that had grown to be somewhat of a status symbol and a privilege for a student to have earned the right to be in it.

"On Wednesday, Chris was diligently working at his desk. I really felt there was a hidden fire deep inside him. I asked Chris if he would like to be in the advanced class. How I wish I could express the look on Chris's face, the

emotions in that shy fourteen-year-old boy, trying to hold
back his tears.

" 'Who, me, Mr. Rowland? Am I good enough?'

" 'Yes, Chris, you are good enough.'

"I had to leave at that point because tears were coming
to my eyes. As Chris walked out of class that day, seemingly two inches taller, he looked at me with bright blue
eyes and said in a positive voice, 'Thank you, Mr.
Rowland.'

"Chris taught me a lesson I will never forget—our deep
desire to feel important. To help me never forget this rule, I
made a sign which reads 'YOU ARE IMPORTANT.' This
sign hangs in the front of the classroom for all to see and to
remind me that each student I face is equally important."

The unvarnished truth is that almost all the people you
meet feel themselves superior to you in some way, and a
sure way to their hearts is to let them realize in some subtle
way that you recognize their importance, and recognize it
sincerely.

Remember what Emerson said: "Every man I meet is
my superior in some way. In that, I learn of him."

And the pathetic part of it is that frequently those who
have the least justification for a feeling of achievement
bolster their egos by a show of tumult and conceit that is
truly nauseating. As Shakespeare put it: " . . . man, proud
man, / Drest in a little brief authority, / . . . Plays such
fantastic tricks before high heaven / As make the angels
weep."

I am going to tell you how business people in my own
courses have applied these principles with remarkable
results. Let's take the case of a Connecticut attorney
(because of his relatives he prefers not to have his name
mentioned).

Shortly after joining the course, Mr. R—— drove to
Long Island with his wife to visit some of her relatives. She

left him to chat with an old aunt of hers and then rushed off by herself to visit some of the younger relatives. Since he soon had to give a speech professionally on how he applied the principles of appreciation, he thought he would gain some worthwhile experience talking with the elderly lady. So he looked around the house to see what he could honestly admire.

"This house was built about 1890, wasn't it?" he inquired.

"Yes," she replied, "that is precisely the year it was built."

"It reminds me of the house I was born in," he said. "It's beautiful. Well built. Roomy. You know, they don't build houses like this anymore."

"You're right," the old lady agreed. "The young folks nowadays don't care for beautiful homes. All they want is a small apartment, and then they go off gadding about in their automobiles.

"This is a dream house," she said in a voice vibrating with tender memories. "This house was built with love. My husband and I dreamed about it for years before we built it. We didn't have an architect. We planned it all ourselves."

She showed Mr. R—— about the house, and he expressed his hearty admiration for the beautiful treasures she had picked up in her travels and cherished over a lifetime—paisley shawls, an old English tea set, Wedgwood china, French beds and chairs, Italian paintings, and silk draperies that had once hung in a French château.

After showing Mr. R—— through the house, she took him out to the garage. There, jacked up on blocks, was a Packard car—in mint condition.

"My husband bought that car for me shortly before he passed on," she said softly. "I have never ridden in it since his death. . . . You appreciate nice things, and I'm going to give this car to you."

"Why, Aunty," he said, "you overwhelm me. I appreciate your generosity, of course; but I couldn't possibly accept it. I'm not even a relative of yours. I have a new car, and you have many relatives who would like to have that Packard."

"Relatives!" she exclaimed. "Yes, I have relatives who are just waiting till I die so they can get that car. But they are not going to get it."

"If you don't want to give it to them, you can very easily sell it to a secondhand dealer," he told her.

"Sell it!" she cried. "Do you think I would sell this car? Do you think I could stand to see strangers riding up and down the street in that car—that car that my husband bought for me? I wouldn't dream of selling it. I'm going to give it to you. You appreciate beautiful things."

He tried to get out of accepting the car, but he couldn't without hurting her feelings.

This lady, left all alone in a big house wth her paisley shawls, her French antiques, and her memories, was starving for a little recognition. She had once been young and beautiful and sought-after. She had once built a house warm with love and had collected things from all over Europe to make it beautiful. Now, in the isolated loneliness of old age, she craved a little human warmth, a little genuine appreciation—and no one gave it to her. And when she found it, like a spring in the desert, her gratitude couldn't adequately express itself with anything less than the gift of her cherished Packard.

Let's take another case: Donald M. McMahon, who was superintendent of Lewis and Valentine, nurserymen and landscape architects in Rye, New York, related this incident:

"Shortly after I attended the talk on 'How to Win Friends and Influence People,' I was landscaping the estate of a famous judge. The owner came out to give me a few instructions about where he wished to plant a mass of rhododendrons and azaleas.

"I said, 'Judge, you have a lovely hobby. I've been admiring your beautiful dogs. I understand you win a lot of blue ribbons every year at the show in Madison Square Garden.'

"The effect of this little expression of appreciation was striking.

" 'Yes,' the judge replied, 'I do have a lot of fun with my dogs. Would you like to see my kennel?'

"He spent almost an hour showing me his dogs and the prizes they had won. He even brought out their pedigrees and explained about the bloodlines responsible for such beauty and intelligence.

"Finally, turning to me, he asked: 'Do you have any small children?'

" 'Yes, I do,' I replied. 'I have a son.'

" 'Well, wouldn't he like a puppy?' the judge inquired.

" 'Oh, yes, he'd be tickled pink.'

" 'All right, I'm going to give him one,' the judge announced.

"He started to tell me how to feed the puppy. Then he paused. 'You'll forget it if I tell you. I'll write it out.' So the judge went in the house, typed out the pedigree and feeding instructions, and gave me a puppy worth several hundred dollars and one hour and fifteen minutes of his valuable time largely because I had expressed my honest admiration for his hobby and achievements."

George Eastman, of Kodak fame, invented the transparent film that made motion pictures possible, amassed a fortune of a hundred million dollars, and made himself one of the most famous businessmen on earth. Yet in spite of all these tremendous accomplishments, he craved a little recognition even as you and I.

To illustrate: When Eastman was building the Eastman School of Music and also Kilbourn Hall in Rochester, James Adamson, then president of the Superior Seating Company of New York, wanted to get the order to supply the theater chairs for these buildings. Phoning the architect, Mr. Adamson made an appointment to see Mr. Eastman in Rochester.

When Adamson arrived, the architect said: "I know you want to get this order, but I can tell you right now that you won't stand a ghost of a show if you take more than five minutes of George Eastman's time. He is a strict disciplinarian. He is very busy. So tell your story quickly and get out."

Adamson was prepared to do just that.

When he was ushered into the room he saw Mr. Eastman bending over a pile of papers at his desk. Presently, Mr. Eastman looked up, removed his glasses, and walked toward the architect and Mr. Adamson, saying: "Good morning, gentlemen, what can I do for you?"

The architect introduced them, and then Mr. Adamson said: "While we've been waiting for you, Mr. Eastman, I've been admiring your office. I wouldn't mind working in a room like this myself. I'm in the interior-woodworking business, and I never saw a more beautiful office in all my life.

George Eastman replied: "You remind me of something I had almost forgotten. It is beautiful, isn't it? I enjoyed it a great deal when it was first built. But I come down here now with a lot of other things on my mind and sometimes don't even see the room for weeks at a time."

Adamson walked over and rubbed his hand across a panel. "This is English oak, isn't it? A little different in texture from Italian oak."

"Yes," Eastman replied. "Imported English oak. It was selected for me by a friend who specializes in fine woods."

Then Eastman showed him about the room, commenting on the proportions, the coloring, the hand carving, and other efforts he had helped to plan and execute.

While drifting about the room, admiring the woodwork, they paused before a window, and George Eastman, in his modest, soft-spoken way, pointed out some of the institutions through which he was trying to help humanity: the University of Rochester, the General Hospital, the Homeopathic Hospital, the Friendly Home, the Children's Hospital. Mr. Adamson congratulated him warmly on the idealistic way he was using his wealth to alleviate the sufferings of humanity. Presently, George Eastman unlocked a glass case and pulled out the first camera he had ever owned—an invention he had bought from an Englishman.

Adamson questioned him at length about his early struggles to get started in business, and Mr. Eastman spoke with real feeling about the poverty of his childhood, telling how his widowed mother had kept a boardinghouse while he clerked in an insurance office. The terror of poverty haunted him day and night, and he resolved to make enough money so that his mother wouldn't have to work. Mr. Adamson drew him out with further questions and listened, absorbed, while he related the story of his experiments with dry photographic plates. He told how he had worked in an office all day, and sometimes experimented all night, taking only brief naps while the chemicals were working and sleeping in his clothes for seventy-two hours at a stretch.

James Adamson had been ushered into Eastman's office at ten-fifteen and had been warned that he must not take more than five minutes; but an hour passed, then two hours passed. And they were still talking.

Finally, George Eastman turned to Adamson and said, "The last time I was in Japan I bought some chairs, brought them home, and put them in my sun porch. But the sun peeled the paint, so I went downtown the other day and bought some paint and painted the chairs myself. Would you like to see what sort of a job I can do painting chairs?

All right. Come up to my home and have lunch with me and I'll show you."

After lunch, Mr. Eastman showed Adamson the chairs he had brought from Japan. They weren't worth more than a few dollars, but George Eastman, now a multimillionaire, was proud of them because he himself had painted them.

The order for the seats amounted to ninety thousand dollars. Who do you suppose got the order—James Adamson or one of his competitors?

From the time of this story until Mr. Eastman's death, he and James Adamson were close friends.

Claude Marais, a restaurant owner in Rouen, France, used this principle and saved his restaurant the loss of a key employee. This woman had been in his employ for five years and was a vital link between M. Marais and his staff of twenty-one people. He was shocked to receive a registered letter from her advising him of her resignation.

M. Marais reported: "I was very surprised and, even more, disappointed, because I was under the impression that I had been fair to her and receptive to her needs. Inasmuch as she was a friend as well as an employee, I probably had taken her too much for granted and maybe was even more demanding of her than of other employees.

"I could not, of course, accept this resignation without some explanation. I took her aside and said, 'Paulette, you must understand that I cannot accept your resignation. You mean a great deal to me and to this company, and you are as important to the success of this restaurant as I am.' I repeated this in front of the entire staff, and I invited her to my home and reiterated my confidence in her with my family present.

"Paulette withdrew her resignation, and today I can rely on her as never before. I frequently reinforce this by expressing my appreciation for what she does and showing her how important she is to me and to the restaurant."

"Talk to people about themselves," said Disraeli, one of the shrewdest men who ever ruled the British Empire. "Talk to people about themselves and they will listen for hours."

Make the other person feel
important—and do it sincerely.

PART THREE

WAYS TO WIN PEOPLE TO YOUR WAY OF THINKING

Dale Carnegie said, "Most men . . . lack [the] subtle ability to enter the citadel of a man's beliefs arm-in-arm with the owner." It is in the development of this subtle ability that the secret lies if you are to learn "How to Win People to Your Way of Thinking and Get Enthusiastic Cooperation."

13

A Sure Way of Making Enemies—and How to Avoid It

When Theodore Roosevelt was in the White House, he confessed that if he could be right seventy-five percent of the time, he would reach the highest measure of his expectation.

If that was the highest rating that one of the most distinguished men of the twentieth century could hope to obtain, what about you and me?

If you can be sure of being right only fifty-five percent of the time, you can go down to Wall Street and make a million dollars a day. If you can't be sure of being right even fifty-five percent of the time, why should you tell other people they are wrong?

You can tell people they are wrong by a look or an intonation or a gesture just as eloquently as you can in words—and if you tell them they are wrong, do you make them want to agree with you? Never! For you have struck a direct blow at their intelligence, judgment, pride, and self-respect. That will make them want to strike back. But it will never make them want to change their minds. You may then hurl at them all the logic of a Plato or an Immanuel Kant, but you will not alter their opinions, for you have hurt their feelings.

Never begin by announcing, "I am going to prove so-and-so to you." That's bad. That's tantamount to saying: "I'm smarter than you are. I'm going to tell you a thing or two and make you change your mind."

That is a challenge. It arouses opposition and makes the listener want to battle with you before you even start. It is difficult, under even the most benign conditions, to change people's minds. So why make it harder? Why handicap yourself?

If you are going to prove anything, don't let anybody know it. Do it so subtly, so adroitly, that no one will feel that you are doing it. This was expressed succinctly by Alexander Pope:

> Men must be taught as if you taught them not
> And things unknown proposed as things forgot.

Over three hundred years ago Galileo said:

> You cannot teach a man anything; you can only help him to find it within himself.

As Lord Chesterfield said to his son:

> Be wiser than other people if you can; but do not tell them so.

Socrates said repeatedly to his followers in Athens:

> One thing only I know, and that is that I know nothing.

Well, I can't hope to be any smarter than Socrates, so I have quit telling people they are wrong. And I find that it pays.

If a person makes a statement that you think is wrong—yes, even that you know is wrong—isn't it better to begin by saying: "Well, now, look. I thought otherwise, but I may be wrong. I frequently am. And If I am wrong, I want to be put right. Let's examine the facts."

There's magic, positive magic, in such phrases as: "I may be wrong. I frequently am. Let's examine the facts."

Nobody in the heavens above or on the earth will ever object to your saying: "I may be wrong. Let's examine the facts."

One of our class members who used this approach in dealing with customers was Harold Reinke, a Dodge dealer in Billings, Montana. He reported that because of the pressures of the automobile business, he was often hard-boiled and callous when dealing with customers' complaints. This caused flared tempers, loss of business, and general unpleasantness.

He told his class: "Recognizing that this was getting me nowhere fast, I tried a new tack. I would say something like this: 'Our dealership has made so many mistakes that I am frequently ashamed. We have erred in your case. Tell me about it.'

"This approach becomes quite disarming, and by the time the customer releases his feelings, he is usually much more reasonable when it comes to settling the matter. In fact, several customers have thanked me for having such an understanding attitude. And two of them have even brought in friends to buy new cars. In this highly competitive market, we need more of this type of customer, and I believe that showing respect for all customers' opinions and treating them diplomatically and courteously will help beat the competition."

You will never get into trouble by admitting that you may be wrong. That will stop all argument and inspire your opponent to be just as fair and open and broad-minded as you are. It will make him want to admit that he, too, may be wrong.

If you know positively that a person is wrong, and you bluntly tell him or her so, what happens? Let me illustrate. Mr. S——, a young New York attorney, once argued a rather important case before the United States Supreme Court (*Lustgarten v. Fleet Corporation 280 U.S. 320*). The case involved a considerable sum of money and an important question of law. During the argument, one of the Supreme Court justices said to him: "The statute of limitations is six years, is it not?"

Mr. S—— stopped, stared at the justice for a moment, and then said bluntly, "Your Honor, there is no statute of limitations in admiralty." .

"A hush fell on the court," said Mr. S—— as he related his experience to one of the author's classes, "and the temperature in the room seemed to drop to zero. I was right. Justice —— was wrong. And I had told him so. But did that make him friendly? No. I still believe that I had the law on my side. And I know that I spoke better than I ever spoke before. But I didn't persuade. I made the enormous blunder of telling a very learned and famous man that he was wrong."

Few people are logical. Most of us are prejudiced and biased. Most of us are blighted with preconceived notions, with jealousy, suspicion, fear, envy, and pride. And most citizens don't want to change their minds about their religion or their haircut or communism or their favorite movie star. So, if you are inclined to tell people they are wrong, please read the following paragraph every morning before breakfast. It is from James Harvey Robinson's enlightening book *The Mind in the Making*.

We sometimes find ourselves changing our minds without any resistance or heavy emotion, but if we are told we are wrong, we resent the imputation and harden our hearts. We are incredibly heedless in the formation of our beliefs, but find ourselves filled with an illicit passion for them when anyone proposes to rob us of their companionship. It is obviously not the ideas themselves that are dear to us, but our self-esteem which is threatened. . . . The little word "my" is the most important one in human affairs, and properly to reckon with it is the beginning of wisdom. It has the same force whether it is "my" dinner, "my" dog, and "my" house, or "my" father, "my" country, and "my" God. We not only resent the imputation that our watch is wrong, or our car shabby, but that our conception of the canals of Mars, of the pronunciation of "Epictetus," of the medicinal value of salicin, or of the date of Sargon I is subject to revision. We like to continue to believe what we have been accustomed to accept as true, and the resentment aroused when doubt is cast upon any of our assumptions leads us to seek every manner of excuse for clinging to it. The result is that most of our so-called reasoning consists in finding arguments for going on believing as we already do.

Carl Rogers, the eminent psychologist, wrote in his book *On Becoming a Person:*

I have found it of enormous value when I can permit myself to understand the other person. The way in which I have worded this statement may seem strange to you. Is it necessary to permit oneself to understand another? I think it is. Our first reaction to most of the statements [which we hear from other people] is an evaluation or judgment, rather than an understanding of it. When someone expresses some feeling, attitude or belief, our tendency is almost immediately to feel "that's right," or "that's stupid," "that's abnormal," "that's unreasonable," "that's incorrect," "that's not nice." Very rarely do we permit ourselves to *understand* precisely what the meaning of the statement is to the other person.*

I once employed an interior decorator to make some draperies for my home. When the bill arrived, I was dismayed.

A few days later, a friend dropped in and looked at the draperies. The price was mentioned, and she exclaimed with a note of triumph: "What? That's awful. I am afraid he put one over on you."

True? Yes, she had told the truth, but few people like to listen to truths that reflect on their judgment. So, being human, I tried to defend myself. I pointed out that the best is eventually the cheapest, that one can't expect to get quality and artistic taste at bargain-basement prices, and so on and on.

The next day another friend dropped in, admired the draperies, bubbled over with enthusiasm, and expressed a wish that she could afford such exquisite creations for her home. My reaction was totally different. "Well, to tell the truth," I said, "I can't afford them myself. I paid too much. I'm sorry I ordered them."

When we are wrong, we may admit it to ourselves. And if we are handled gently and tactfully, we may admit it to others and even take pride in our frankness and broad-

*Adapted from Carl Rogers, *On Becoming a Person* (Boston: Houghton Mifflin, 1961), pp. 18ff.

mindedness. But not if someone else is trying to ram the unpalatable fact down our esophagus.

Horace Greeley, the most famous editor in America during the time of the Civil War, disagreed violently with Lincoln's policies. He believed that he could drive Lincoln into agreeing with him by a campaign of argument, ridicule, and abuse. He waged this bitter campaign month after month, year after year. In fact, he wrote a brutal, bitter, sarcastic, and personal attack on President Lincoln the night Booth shot him.

But did all this bitterness make Lincoln agree with Greeley? Not at all. Ridicule and abuse never do.

If you want some excellent suggestions about dealing with people and managing yourself and improving your personality, read Benjamin Franklin's autobiography—one of the most fascinating life stories ever written, one of the classics of American literature. Ben Franklin tells how he conquered the iniquitous habit of argument and transformed himself into one of the most able, suave, and diplomatic men in American history.

One day, when Ben Franklin was a blundering youth, an old Quaker friend took him aside and lashed him with a few stinging truths, something like this:

Ben, you are impossible. Your opinions have a slap in them for everyone who differs with you. They have become so offensive that nobody cares for them. Your friends find they enjoy themselves better when you are not around. You know so much that no man can tell you anything. Indeed, no man is going to try, for the effort would lead only to discomfort and hard work. So you are not likely ever to know any more than you do now, which is very little.

One of the finest things I know about Ben Franklin is the way he accepted that smarting rebuke. He was big enough and wise enough to realize that it was true, to sense that he was headed for failure and social disaster. So he made a right-about-face. He began immediately to change his insolent, opinionated ways.

"I made it a rule," said Franklin, "to forbear all direct contradiction to the sentiment of others, and all positive assertion of my own. I even forbade myself the use of every word or expression in the language that imported a fix'd opinion, such as 'certainly,' 'undoubtedly,' etc., and I adopted, instead of them, 'I conceive,' 'I apprehend,' or 'I imagine' a thing to be so or so, or 'it so appears to me at present.' When another asserted something that I thought an error, I deny'd myself the pleasure of contradicting him abruptly, and of showing immediately some absurdity in his proposition: and in answering I began by observing that in certain cases or instances his opinion would be right, but in the present case there appear'd or seem'd to me some difference, etc. I soon found the advantage of this change in my manner; the conversations I engag'd in went on more pleasantly. The modest way in which I propos'd my opinions procur'd them a readier reception and less contradiction; I had less mortification when I was found to be in the wrong, and I more easily prevail'd with others to give up their mistakes and join with me when I happened to be in the right.

"And this mode, which I at first put on with some violence to natural inclination, became at length so easy, and so habitual to me, that perhaps for these fifty years past no one has ever heard a dogmatical expression escape me. And to this habit (after my character of integrity) I think it principally owing that I had earned so much weight with my fellow citizens when I proposed new institutions, or alterations in the old, and so much influence in public councils when I became a member; for I was but a bad speaker, never eloquent, subject to much hesitation in my choice of words, hardly correct in language, and yet I generally carried my points."

How do Ben Franklin's methods work in business? Let's take two examples.

Katherine A. Allred of Kings Mountain, North Carolina, is an industrial engineering supervisor for a yarn-processing plant. She told one of our classes how she handled a sensitive problem before and after taking our training:

"Part of my responsibility," she reported, "deals with setting up and maintaining incentive systems and standards for our operators so they can make more money by producing more yarn. The system we were using had worked fine when we had only two or three different types of yarn, but recently we had expanded our inventory and capabilities to enable us to run more than twelve different varieties. The present system was no longer adequate to pay the operators fairly for the work being performed and give them an incentive to increase production. I had worked up a new system which would enable us to pay the operator by the class of yarn she was running at any one particular time. With my new system in hand, I entered the meeting determined to prove to the management that my system was the right approach. I told them in detail how they were wrong and showed where they were being unfair and how I had all the answers they needed. To say the least, I failed miserably! I had become so busy defending my position on the new system that I had left them no opening to graciously admit their problems on the old one. The issue was dead.

"After several sessions of this course, I realized all too well where I had made my mistakes. I called another meeting and this time I asked where they felt their problems were. We discussed each point, and I asked them their opinions on which was the best way to proceed. With a few low-keyed suggestions, at proper intervals, I let them develop my system themselves. At the end of the meeting when I actually presented my system, they enthusiastically accepted it.

"I am convinced now that nothing good is accomplished and a lot of damage can be done if you tell a person straight out that he or she is wrong. You only succeed in stripping that person of self-dignity and making yourself an unwelcome part of any discussion."

Let's take another example—and remember these cases I am citing are typical of the experiences of thousands of other people. R. V. Crowley was a salesman for a lumber company in New York. Crowley admitted that he had been telling hard-boiled lumber inspectors for years that they were wrong. And he had won the arguments too. But it hadn't done any good. "For these lumber inspectors," said Mr. Crowley, "are like baseball umpires. Once they make a decision, they never change it."

Mr. Crowley saw that his firm was losing thousands of dollars through the arguments he won. So while taking my course, he resolved to change tactics and abandon arguments. With what results? Here is the story as he told it to the fellow members of his class:

"One morning the phone rang in my office. A hot and bothered person at the other end proceeded to inform me that a car of lumber we had shipped into his plant was entirely unsatisfactory. His firm had stopped unloading and requested that we make immediate arrangements to remove the stock from their yard. After about one-fourth of the car had been unloaded, their lumber inspector reported that the lumber was running fifty-five percent below grade. Under the circumstances, they refused to accept it.

"I immediately started for his plant and on the way turned over in my mind the best way to handle the situation. Ordinarily, under such circumstances, I should have quoted grading rules and tried, as a result of my own experience and knowledge as a lumber inspector, to convince the other inspector that the lumber was actually up to grade, and that he was misinterpreting the rules in his inspection. However, I thought I would apply the principles learned in this training.

"When I arrived at the plant, I found the purchasing agent and the lumber inspector in a wicked humor, both set for an argument and a fight. We walked out to the car that was being unloaded, and I requested that they continue to unload so that I could see how things were going. I asked the inspector to go right ahead and lay out the rejects, as he had been doing, and to put the good pieces in another pile.

"After watching him for a while it began to dawn on me that his inspection actually was much too strict and that he was misinterpreting the rules. This particular lumber was white pine, and I knew the inspector was thoroughly schooled in hard woods but not a competent, experienced inspector on white pine. White pine happened to be my own strong suit, but did I offer any objection to the way he was grading the lumber? None whatever. I kept on watching and gradually began to ask questions as to why certain pieces were not satisfactory. I didn't for one instant insinuate that the inspector was wrong. I emphasized that my only reason for asking was in order that we could give his firm exactly what they wanted in future shipments.

"By asking questions in a very friendly, cooperative spirit, and insisting continually that they were right in laying out boards not satisfactory to their purpose, I got him warmed up, and the strained relations between us began to thaw and melt away. An occasional carefully put remark on my part gave birth to the idea in his mind that possibly some of these rejected pieces were actually within the grade that they had bought, and that their requirements demanded a more expensive grade. I was very careful, however, not to let him think I was making an issue of this point.

"Gradually his whole attitude changed: He finally admitted to me that he was not experienced on white pine and began to ask me questions about each piece as it came out of the car. I would explain why such a piece came within the grade specified, but kept on insisting that we did not want him to take it if it was unsuitable for their purpose. He finally got to the point where he felt guilty every time he put a piece in the rejected pile. And at last he saw that the mistake was on their part for not having specified as good a grade as they needed.

"The ultimate outcome was that he went through the entire carload again after I left, accepted the whole lot, and we received a check in full.

"In that one instance alone, a little tact, and the determination to refrain from telling the other man he was wrong, saved my company a substantial amount of cash, and it would be hard to place a money value on the good will that was saved."

Martin Luther King, Jr., was asked how, as a pacifist, he could be an admirer of Air Force General Daniel "Chappie" James, then the nation's highest-ranking black officer. Dr. King replied, "I judge people by their own principles—not by my own."

In a similar way, General Robert E. Lee once spoke to the president of the Confederacy, Jefferson Davis, in the most glowing terms about a certain officer under his command. Another officer was astonished. "General," he said, "do you not know that the man of whom you speak so highly is one of your bitterest enemies who misses no opportunity to malign you?" "Yes," replied General Lee, "but the president asked my opinion of him; he did not ask for his opinion of me."

By the way, I am not revealing anything new in this chapter. Two thousand years ago, Jesus said: "Agree with thine adversary quickly."

And twenty-two hundred years before Christ was born, Pharaoh Akhtoi of Egypt gave his son some shrewd advice—advice that is sorely needed today. "Be diplomatic," counseled the pharaoh. "It will help you gain your point."

In other words, don't argue with your customer or your spouse or your adversary. Don't tell them they are wrong, don't get them stirred up. Use a little diplomacy.

Show respect for the other person's opinions. Never say, "You're wrong."

14

The High Road to Reason

If your temper is aroused and you tell 'em a thing or two, you will have a fine time unloading your feelings. But what about the other person? Will he share your pleasure? Will your belligerent tones, your hostile attitude, make it easy for him to agree with you?

"If you come at me with your fists doubled," said Woodrow Wilson, "I think I can promise you that mine will double as fast as yours; but if you come to me and say, 'Let us sit down and take counsel together, and, if we differ from each other, understand why it is that we differ, just what the points at issue are,' we will presently find that we are not so far apart after all, that the points on which we differ are few and the points on which we agree are many, and that if we only have the patience and the candor and the desire to get together, we will get together."

Nobody appreciated the truth of Woodrow Wilson's statement more than John D. Rockefeller, Jr. Back in 1915, Rockefeller was the most fiercely despised man in Colorado. One of the bloodiest strikes in the history of American industry had been shocking the state for two terrible years. Irate, belligerent miners were demanding higher wages from the Colorado Fuel and Iron Company; Rockefeller controlled that company. Property had been destroyed, troops had been called out. Blood had been shed. Strikers had been shot, their bodies riddled with bullets.

At a time like that, with the air seething with hatred, Rockefeller wanted to win the strikers to his way of thinking. And he did it. How? Here's the story. After weeks spent in making friends, Rockefeller addressed the representatives of the strikers. This speech, in its entirety, is a masterpiece. It produced astonishing results. It calmed the tempestuous waves of hate that threatened to engulf Rockefeller. It won him a host of admirers. It presented facts in such a friendly manner that the strikers went back to work without saying another word about the increase in wages for which they had fought so violently.

The opening of that remarkable speech follows. Note how it fairly glows with friendliness. Rockefeller, remember, was talking to men who, a few days previously, had wanted to hang him by the neck to a sour apple tree; yet he couldn't have been more gracious, more friendly if he had addressed a group of medical missionaries. His speech was radiant with such phrases as I am *proud* to be here, having *visited* in *your homes*, met many of your wives and children, we meet here not as strangers, but as *friends* . . . spirit of *mutual friendship*, our *common interests*, it is only by *your courtesy* that I am here.

"This is a red-letter day in my life," Rockefeller began. "It is the first time I have ever had the good fortune to meet the representatives of the employees of this great company, its officers and superintendents, together, and I can assure you that I am proud to be here, and that I shall remember this gathering as long as I live. Had this meeting been held two weeks ago, I should have stood here a stranger to most of you, recognizing a few faces. Having had the opportunity last week of visiting all the camps in the southern coal field and of talking individually with practically all of the

representatives, except those who were away; having visited in your homes, met many of your wives and children,
we meet here not as strangers, but as friends, and it is in
that spirit of mutual friendship that I am glad to have this
opportunity to discuss with you our common interests.

"Since this is a meeting of the officers of the company
and the representatives of the employees, it is only by your
courtesy that I am here, for I am not so fortunate as to be
either one or the other; and yet I feel that I am intimately
associated with you men, for, in a sense, I represent both
the stockholders and the directors."

Isn't that a superb example of the fine art of making
friends out of enemies?

Suppose Rockefeller had taken a different tack. Suppose he had argued with these miners and hurled devastating facts in their faces. Suppose he had told them by his
tone and insinuations that they were wrong. Suppose that,
by all the rules of logic, he had proved that they were
wrong. What would have happened? More anger would
have been stirred up, more hatred, more revolt.

> If a man's heart is rankling with discord and ill
> feeling toward you, you can't win him to your way
> of thinking with all the logic in Christendom. Scold-
> ing parents and domineering bosses and husbands
> and nagging wives ought to realize that people don't
> want to change their minds. They can't be forced or
> driven to agree with you or me. But they may
> possibly be led to, if we are gentle and friendly, ever
> so gentle and ever so friendly.

Lincoln said that, in effect, over a hundred years ago.
Here are his words:

> It is an old and true maxim that "a drop of honey
> catches more flies than a gallon of gall." So with

men, if you would win a man to your cause, first
convince him that you are his sincere friend.
Therein is a drop of honey that catches his heart;
which, say what you will, is the great high road to
his reason.

Business executives have learned that it pays to be
friendly to strikers. For example, when twenty-five hundred employees in the White Motor Company's plant
struck for higher wages and a union shop, Robert F. Black,
then president of the company, didn't lose his temper and
condemn and threaten and talk of tyranny and communists.
He actually praised the strikers. He published an advertise-
ment in the Cleveland papers, complimenting them on "the
peaceful way in which they laid down their tools." Finding
the strike pickets idle, he bought them a couple of dozen
baseball bats and gloves and invited them to play ball on
vacant lots. For those who preferred bowling, he rented a
bowling alley.

This friendliness on Mr. Black's part did what friendliness always does: it begot friendliness. So the strikers
borrowed brooms, shovels, and rubbish carts, and began
picking up matches, papers, cigarette stubs, and cigar butts
around the factory. Imagine it! Imagine strikers tidying up
the factory grounds while battling for higher wages and
recognition of the union. Such an event had never been
heard of before in the long, tempestuous history of American labor wars. That strike ended with a compromise
settlement within a week—ended without any ill feeling or
rancor.

Daniel Webster, who looked like a god and talked like
Jehovah, was one of the most successful advocates who
ever pleaded a case; yet he ushered in his most powerful
arguments with such friendly remarks as: "It will be for the
jury to consider," "This may, perhaps, be worth thinking
of," "Here are some facts that I trust you will not lose sight

of," or "You, with your knowledge of human nature, will easily see the significance of these facts." No bulldozing. No high-pressure methods. No attempt to force his opinions on others. Webster used the soft-spoken, quiet, friendly approach, and it helped to make him famous.

You may never be called upon to settle a strike or address a jury, but you may want to get your rent reduced. Will the friendly approach help you then? Let's see.

O. L. Straub, an engineer, wanted to get his rent reduced. And he knew his landlord was hard-boiled. "I wrote him," Mr. Straub said in a speech before the class, "notifying him that I was vacating my apartment as soon as my lease expired. The truth was, I didn't want to move. I wanted to stay if I could get my rent reduced. But the situation seemed hopeless. Other tenants had tried—and failed. Everyone told me that the landlord was extremely difficult to deal with. But I said to myself, 'I am studying a course in how to deal with people, so I'll try it on him—and see how it works.'

"He and his secretary came to see me as soon as he got my letter. I met him at the door with a friendly greeting. I fairly bubbled with good will and enthusiasm. I didn't begin talking about how high the rent was. I began talking about how much I liked his apartment house. Believe me, I was 'hearty in my approbation and lavish in my praise.' I complimented him on the way he ran the building and told him I should like so much to stay for another year but I couldn't afford it.

"He had evidently never had such a reception from a tenant. He hardly knew what to make of it.

"Then he started to tell me his troubles. Complaining tenants. One had written him fourteen letters, some of them positively insulting. Another threatened to break his lease unless the landlord kept the man on the floor above from snoring. 'What a relief it is,' he said, 'to have a satisfied tenant like you.' And then, without my even asking him to do it, he offered to reduce my rent a little. I wanted more, so I named the figure I could afford to pay, and he accepted without a word.

"As he was leaving, he turned to me and asked, 'What decorating can I do for you?'

"If I had tried to get the rent reduced by the methods the other tenants were using, I am positive I should have met the same failure they encountered. It was the friendly, sympathetic, appreciative approach that won."

Dean Woodcock of Pittsburgh, Pennsylvania, is the superintendent of a department of the local electric company. His staff was called upon to repair some equipment on top of a pole. This type of work had formerly been performed by a different department and had only recently been transferred to Woodcock's section. Although his people had been trained in the work, this was the first time they had ever actually been called upon to do it. Everybody in the organization was interested in seeing if and how they could handle it. Mr. Woodcock, several of his subordinate managers, and members of other departments of the utility went to see the operation. Many cars and trucks were there, and a number of people were standing around watching the two lone men on top of the pole.

Glancing around, Woodcock noticed a man up the street getting out of his car with a camera. He began taking pictures of the scene. Utility people are extremely conscious of public relations, and suddenly Woodcock realized what this setup looked like to the man with the camera—overkill, dozens of people being called out to do a two-person job. He strolled up the street to the photographer.

"I see you're interested in our operation."

"Yes, and my mother will be more than interested. She owns stock in your company. This will be an eye-opener for her. She may even decide her investment was unwise. I've been telling her for years there's a lot of waste motion in companies like yours. This proves it. The newspapers might like these pictures, too."

"It does look like it, doesn't it? I'd think the same thing in your position. But this is a unique situation, . . ." and Dean Woodcock went on to explain how this was the first job of this type for his department and how everyone from executives down was interested. He assured the man that under normal conditions two people could handle the job. The photographer put away his camera, shook Woodcock's hand, and thanked him for taking the time to explain the situation to him.

Dean Woodcock's friendly approach saved his company much embarrassment and bad publicity.

Another member of one of our classes, Gerald H. Winn of Littleton, New Hampshire, reported how, by using a friendly approach, he obtained a very satisfactory settlement on a damage claim.

"Early in the spring," he reported, "before the ground had thawed from winter freezing, there was an unusually heavy rainstorm and the water, which normally would have run off to nearby ditches and storm drains along the road, took a new course onto a building lot where I had just built a new home.

"Not being able to run off, the water pressure built up around the foundation of the house. The water forced itself under the concrete basement floor, causing it to explode, and the basement filled with water. This ruined the furnace and the hot-water heater. The cost to repair this damage was in excess of two thousand dollars. I had no insurance to cover this type of damage.

"However, I soon found out that the owner of the subdivision had neglected to put in a storm drain near the house which could have prevented this problem. I made an appointment to see him. During the twenty-five-minute trip to his office, I carefully reviewed the situation and, remembering the principles I learned in this course, I decided that showing my anger would not serve any worthwhile purpose. When I arrived, I kept very calm and started by talking about his recent vacation to the West Indies; then, when I felt the timing was right, I mentioned the 'little' problem of water damage. He quickly agreed to do his share in helping to correct the problem.

"A few days later he called and said he would pay for the damage and also put in a storm drain to prevent the same thing from happening in the future.

"Even though it was the fault of the owner of the subdivision, if I had not begun in a friendly way, there would have been a great deal of difficulty in getting him to agree to the total liability."

Years ago, when I was a barefoot boy walking through the woods to a country school out in northwest Missouri, I read a fable by Aesop about the sun and the wind. They quarreled about which was the stronger, and the wind said, "I'll prove I am. See the old man down there with a coat? I bet I can get his coat off him quicker than you can."

So the sun went behind a cloud, and the wind blew until it was almost a tornado, but the harder it blew, the tighter the old man clutched his coat to him.

Finally, the wind calmed down and gave up, and then the sun came out from behind the clouds and smiled kindly on the old man. Presently, he mopped his brow and pulled off his coat. The sun then told the wind that gentleness and friendliness were always stronger than fury and force.

The use of gentleness and friendliness is demonstrated day after day by people who have learned that a drop of honey catches more flies than a gallon of gall. F. Gale Connor of Lutherville, Maryland, proved this when he had to take his four-month-old car to the service department of the car dealer for the third time. He told our class: "It was apparent that talking to, reasoning with, or shouting at the service manager was not going to lead to a satisfactory resolution of my problems.

"I walked over to the showroom and asked to see the agency owner, Mr. White. After a short wait, I was ushered into Mr. White's office. I introduced myself and explained to him that I had bought my car from his dealership because of the recommendations of friends who had had previous dealings with him. I was told that his prices were very competitive and his service was outstanding. He smiled with satisfaction as he listened to me. I then explained the problem I was having with the service department. 'I thought you might want to be aware of any situation that might tarnish your fine reputation,' I added. He thanked me for calling this to his attention and assured me that my problem would be taken care of. Not only did he personally get involved, but he also lent me his car to use while mine was being repaired."

Aesop was a Greek slave who lived at the court of Croesus and spun immortal fables six hundred years before Christ. Yet the truths he taught about human nature are just as true in Boston and Birmingham now as they were twenty-six centuries ago in Athens. The sun can make you take off your coat more quickly than the wind; and kindliness, the friendly approach, and appreciation can make people change their minds more readily than all the bluster and storming in the world.

Remember what Lincoln said: "A drop of honey catches more flies than a gallon of gall."

Begin in a friendly way.

15

The Secret of Socrates

In talking with other people, don't begin by discussing the things on which you differ. Begin by emphasizing—and keep on emphasizing—the things on which you agree. Keep emphasizing, if possible, that you are both striving for the same end and that your only difference is one of method and not of purpose.

Get the other person saying "Yes, yes" at the outset. Keep your opponent, if possible, from saying "No."

A "No" response, according to Professor Harry Overstreet,* is a most difficult handicap to overcome. When you have said "No," all your pride of personality demands that you remain consistent with yourself. You may later feel that the "No" was ill-advised; nevertheless, there is your precious pride to consider! Once having said a thing, you feel you must stick to it. Hence it is of the very greatest importance that a person be started in the affirmative direction.

The skillful speaker gets, at the outset, a number of "Yes" responses. This sets the psychological process of the listeners moving in the affirmative direction. It is like

*Harry A. Overstreet, *Influencing Human Behavior* (New York: Norton, 1925).

the movement of a billiard ball. Propel it one direction, and it takes some force to deflect it, far more force to send it back in the opposite direction.

The psychological patterns here are quite clear. When a person says "No" and really means it, he or she is doing far more than saying a word of two letters. The entire organism—glandular, nervous, muscular—gathers itself together into a condition of rejection. There is, usually in minute but sometimes in observable degree, a physical withdrawal or readiness for withdrawal. The whole neuromuscular system, in short, sets itself on guard against acceptance. When, to the contrary, a person says "Yes," none of the withdrawal activities takes place. The organism is in a forward-moving, accepting, open attitude. Hence the more Yeses we can, at the very outset, induce, the more likely we are to succeed in capturing the attention for our ultimate proposal.

It is a very simple technique—this "Yes" response. And yet, how much it is neglected! It often seems as if people get a sense of their own importance by antagonizing others at the outset.

Get a student to say "No" at the beginning, or a customer, child, husband, or wife, and it takes the wisdom and the patience of angels to transform that bristling negative into an affirmative.

The use of this "Yes, yes" technique enabled James Eberson, who was a teller at the Greenwich Savings Bank, in New York City, to secure a prospective customer who might otherwise have been lost.

"This man came in to open an account," said Mr. Eberson, "and I gave him our usual form to fill out. Some of the questions he answered willingly, but there were others he flatly refused to answer.

"Before I began the study of human relations, I would have told this prospective depositor that if he refused to give the bank this information, we should have to refuse to accept his account. I am ashamed that I have been guilty of doing that very thing in the past. Naturally, an ultimatum like that made me feel good. I had shown who was boss, that the bank's rules and regulations couldn't be flouted. But that sort of attitude certainly didn't give a feeling of welcome and importance to the man who had walked in to give us his patronage.

"I resolved this morning to use a little horse sense. I resolved not to talk about what the bank wanted but about what the customer wanted. And above all else, I was determined to get him saying 'Yes, yes' from the very start. So I agreed with him. I told him the information he refused to give was not absolutely necessary.

" 'However,' I said, 'suppose you have money in this bank at your death. Wouldn't you like to have the bank transfer it to your next of kin, who is entitled to it according to law?'

" 'Yes, of course,' he replied.

" 'Don't you think,' I continued, 'that it would be a good idea to give us the name of your next of kin so that, in the event of your death, we could carry out your wishes without error or delay?'

"Again he said, 'Yes.'

"The young man's attitude softened and changed when he realized that we weren't asking for this information for our sake but for his sake. Before leaving the bank, this young man not only gave me complete information about himself but he opened, at my suggestion, a trust account, naming his mother as the beneficiary for his account, and he had gladly answered all the questions concerning his mother also.

"I found that by getting him to say 'Yes, yes' from the outset, he forgot the issue at stake and was happy to do all the things I suggested."

Joseph Allison, a sales representative for Westinghouse Electric Company, had this story to tell: "There was a man in my territory that our company was most eager to sell to. My predecessor had called on him for ten years without selling anything. When I took over the territory, I called steadily for three years without getting an order. Finally, after thirteen years of calls and sales talk, we sold him a few motors. If these proved to be all right, an order for several hundred more would follow. Such was my expectation.

"Right? I knew they would be all right. So when I called three weeks later, I was in high spirits.

"The chief engineer greeted me with this shocking announcement: 'Allison, I can't buy the remainder of the motors from you.'

" 'Why?' I asked in amazement. 'Why?'

" 'Because your motors are too hot. I can't put my hand on them.'

"I knew it wouldn't do any good to argue. I had tried that sort of thing too long. So I thought of getting the 'Yes, yes' response.

" 'Well, now, look, Mr. Smith,' I said. 'I agree with you a hundred percent; if those motors are running too hot, you ought not to buy any more of them. You must have motors that won't run any hotter than standards set by the National Electrical Manufacturers Association. Isn't that so?'

"He agreed it was. I had gotten my first 'yes.'

" 'The Electrical Manufacturers Association regulations say that a properly designed motor may have a temperature of 72 degrees Fahrenheit above room temperature. Is that correct?'

" 'Yes,' he agreed. 'That's quite correct. But your motors are much hotter.'

"I didn't argue with him. I merely asked, 'How hot is the mill room?'

" 'Oh,' he said, 'about 75 degrees Fahrenheit.'

" 'Well,' I replied, 'if the mill room is 75 degrees and you add 72 to that, that makes a total of 147 degrees Fahrenheit. Wouldn't you scald your hand if you held it under a spigot of hot water at a temperature of 147 degrees Fahrenheit?'

"Again he had to say 'Yes.'

" 'Well,' I suggested, 'wouldn't it be a good idea to keep your hands off those motors?'

" 'Well, I guess you're right,' he admitted. We continued to chat for a while. Then he called his secretary and lined up approximately thirty-five thousand dollars worth of business for the ensuing month.

"It took me years and cost me countless thousands of dollars in lost business before I finally learned that it doesn't pay to argue, that it is much more profitable and much more interesting to look at things from the other person's viewpoint and try to get that person saying 'Yes, yes.' "

Eddie Snow, who sponsors our courses in Oakland, California, tells how he became a good customer of a shop because the proprietor got him to say "Yes, yes." Eddie had become interested in bow-and-arrow hunting and had spent considerable money in purchasing equipment and supplies from a local store. When his brother was visiting him he wanted to rent a bow for him from this store. The sales clerk told him they didn't rent bows, so Eddie phoned another store. Eddie described what happened:

"A very pleasant gentleman answered the phone. His response to my question for a rental was completely different from the other place. He said he was sorry but they no longer rented bows because they couldn't afford to do so. He then asked me if I had rented before. I replied, 'Yes, several years ago.' He reminded me that I probably paid $25 to $30 for the rental. I said 'Yes' again. He then asked if I was the kind of person who liked to save money. Naturally, I answered 'Yes.' He went on to explain that they had bow sets with all the necessary equipment on sale for $34.95. I could buy a complete set for only $4.95 more than the cost of renting one. He explained that is why they had discontinued renting them. Did I think that was reasonable? My 'Yes' response led to a purchase of the set, and when I picked it up I purchased several more items at this shop and have since become a regular customer."

Socrates, the "gadfly of Athens," was one of the greatest philosophers the world has ever known. He did something that only a handful of men in all history have been able to do: he sharply changed the whole course of human thought; and now, twenty-four centuries after his death, he is honored as one of the wisest persuaders who ever influenced the wrangling world.

His method? Did he tell people they were wrong? Oh, no, not Socrates. He was far too adroit for that. His whole technique, now called the "Socratic method," was based upon getting a "Yes, yes" response. He asked questions with which his opponents would have to agree. He kept on winning one admission after another until he had an armful of yeses. He kept on asking questions until finally, almost without realizing it, his opponents found themselves embracing a conclusion they would have bitterly denied a few minutes previously.

The next time we are tempted to tell someone he or she is wrong, let's remember Socrates and ask a gentle question—a question that will get the "Yes, yes" response.

The Chinese have a proverb pregnant with the age-old wisdom of the Orient: "He who treads softly goes far."

They have spent five thousand years studying human nature, those cultured Chinese, and they have garnered a lot of perspicacity: *"He who treads softly goes far."*

**Get the other person saying "Yes, yes"
immediately.**

16

How to Get Cooperation

Don't you have much more faith in ideas that you discover for yourself than in ideas that are handed to you on a silver platter? If so, isn't it bad judgment to try to ram your opinions down the throats of other people? Isn't it wiser to make suggestions—and let the other person think out the conclusion?

Adolph Seltz of Philadelphia, sales manager in an automobile showroom and a student in one of my courses, suddenly found himself confronted with the necessity of injecting enthusiasm into a discouraged and disorganized group of automobile salespeople. Calling a sales meeting, he urged his people to tell him exactly what they expected from him. As they talked, he wrote their ideas on the blackboard. He then said: "I'll give you all these qualities you expect from me. Now I want you to tell me what I have a right to expect from you." The replies came quick and fast: loyalty, honesty, initiative, optimism, teamwork, eight hours a day of enthusiastic work. The meeting ended with a new courage, a new inspiration—one salesperson volunteered to work fourteen hours a day—and Mr. Seltz reported to me that the increase of sales was phenomenal.

"The people had made a sort of moral bargain with

me," said Mr. Seltz, "and as long as I lived up to my part in it, they were determined to live up to theirs. Consulting them about their wishes and desires was just the shot in the arm they needed."

No one likes to feel that he or she is being sold something or told to do a thing. We much prefer to feel that we are buying of our own accord or acting on our own ideas. We like to be consulted about our wishes, our wants, our thoughts.

Take the case of Eugene Wesson. He lost countless thousands of dollars in commissions before he learned this truth. Mr. Wesson sold sketches for a studio that created designs for stylists and textile manufacturers. Mr. Wesson had called on one of the leading stylists in New York once a week, every week for three years. "He never refused to see me," said Mr. Wesson, "but he never bought. He always looked over my sketches very carefully and then said: 'No, Wesson, I guess we don't get together today.' "

After 150 failures, Wesson realized he must be in a mental rut, so he resolved to devote one evening a week to the study of influencing human behavior, to help him develop new ideas and generate new enthusiasm.

He decided on this new approach. With half a dozen unfinished artists' sketches under his arm, he rushed over to the buyer's office. "I want you to do me a little favor, if you will," he said. "Here are some uncompleted sketches. Won't you please tell me how we could finish them up in such a way that you could use them?"

The buyer looked at the sketches for a while without uttering a word. Finally he said: "Leave these with me for a few days, Wesson, and then come back and see me."

Wesson returned three days later, got his suggestions, took the sketches back to the studio, and had them finished according to the buyer's ideas. The result? All accepted.

After that, this buyer ordered scores of other sketches

from Wesson, all drawn according to the buyer's ideas. "I realized why I had failed for years to sell him," said Mr. Wesson. "I had urged him to buy what I thought he ought to have. Then I changed my approach completely. I urged him to give me his ideas. This made him feel that he was creating the designs. And he was. I didn't have to sell him. He bought."

Letting the other person feel that the idea is his or hers not only works in business and politics, it works in family life as well. Paul M. Davis of Tulsa, Oklahoma, told his class how he applied this principle:

"My family and I enjoyed one of the most interesting sightseeing vacation trips we have ever taken. I had long dreamed of visiting such historic sites as the Civil War battlefield in Gettysburg, Independence Hall in Philadelphia, and our nation's capital. Valley Forge, Jamestown, and the restored colonial village of Williamsburg were high on the list of things I wanted to see.

"In March my wife, Nancy, mentioned that she had ideas for our summer vacation which included a tour of the western states, visiting points of interest in New Mexico, Arizona, California, and Nevada. She had wanted to make this trip for several years. But we couldn't, obviously, make both trips.

"Our daughter, Anne, had just completed a course in U.S. history in junior high school and had become very interested in the events that shaped our country's growth. I asked her how she would like to visit the places she had learned about on our next vacation. She said she would love to.

"Two evenings later as we sat around the dinner table, Nancy announced that if we all agreed, the summer's vacation would be to the eastern states, that it would be a great trip for Anne and thrilling for all of us. We all concurred."

This same psychology was used by an X-ray manufacturer to sell his equipment to one of the largest hospitals in Brooklyn. This hospital was building an addition and preparing to equip it with the finest X-ray department in America. Dr. L——, who was in charge of the X-ray department, was overwhelmed with sales representatives, each caroling the praises of his own company's equipment.

One manufacturer, however, was more skillful. He knew far more about handling human nature than the others did. He wrote a letter something like this:

Our factory has recently completed a new line of X-ray equipment. The first shipment of these machines has just arrived at our office. They are not perfect. We know that, and we want to improve them. So we should be deeply obligated to you if you could find time to look them over and give us your ideas about how they can be made more serviceable to your profession. Knowing how occupied you are, I shall be glad to send my car for you at any hour you specify.

"I was surprised to get that letter," Dr. L—— said as he related the incident before the class. "I was both surprised and complimented. I had never had an X-ray manufacturer seeking my advice before. It made me feel important. I was busy every night that week, but I canceled a dinner appointment in order to look over the equipment. The more I studied it, the more I discovered for myself how much I liked it.

"Nobody had tried to sell it to me. I felt that the idea of buying that equipment for the hospital was my own. I sold myself on its superior qualities and ordered it installed."

Ralph Waldo Emerson in his essay "Self-Reliance" stated: "In every work of genius we recognize our own rejected thoughts; they come back to us with a certain alienated majesty."

Colonel Edward M. House wielded an enormous influence in national and international affairs while Woodrow Wilson occupied the White House. Wilson leaned upon Colonel House for secret counsel and advice more than he did upon even members of his own cabinet.

What method did the colonel use in influencing the President? Fortunately, we know, for House himself revealed it to Arthur D. Howden Smith, and Smith quoted House in an article in *The Saturday Evening Post*.

" 'After I got to know the President,' House said, 'I learned the best way to convert him to an idea was to plant it in his mind casually, but so as to interest him in it—so as to get him thinking about it on his own account. The first time this worked it was an accident. I had been visiting him at the White House and urged a policy on him which he appeared to disapprove. But several days later, at the dinner table, I was amazed to hear him trot out my suggestion as his own.' "

Did House interrupt him and say, "That's not your idea. That's mine"? Oh, no. Not House. He was too adroit for that. He didn't care about credit. He wanted results. So he let Wilson continue to feel that the idea was his. House did even more than that. He gave Wilson public credit for these ideas.

Let's remember that everyone we come in contact with is just as human as Woodrow Wilson. So let's use Colonel House's technique.

A man up in the beautiful Canadian province of New Brunswick used this technique on me and won my patronage. I was planning at the time to do some fishing and canoeing in New Brunswick. So I wrote the tourist bureau for information. Evidently my name and address were put on a mailing list, for I was immediately overwhelmed with scores of letters and booklets and printed testimonials from camps and guides. I was bewildered. I didn't know which to choose. Then one camp owner did a clever thing. He sent me the names and telephone numbers of several New York people who had stayed at his camp and he invited me to telephone them and discover for myself what he had to offer.

I found to my surprise that I knew one of the men on his list. I telephoned him, found out what his experience had been, and then wired the camp the date of my arrival.

The others had been trying to sell me their service, but one let me sell myself. That organization won.

Twenty-five centuries ago, Lao-tse, a Chinese sage, said some things that readers of this book might use today:

"The reason why rivers and seas receive the homage of a hundred mountain streams is that they keep below them. Thus they are able to reign over all the mountain streams. So the sage, wishing to be above men, putteth himself below them; wishing to be before them, he putteth himself behind them. Thus, though his place be above men, they do not feel his weight; though his place be before them, they do not count it an injury."

Let the other person feel that the idea is his or hers.

17

An Appeal That Everybody Likes

I was reared on the edge of the Jesse James country out in Missouri, and I visited the James farm at Kearney, Missouri, where the son of Jesse James was then living.

His wife told me stories of how Jesse robbed trains and held up banks and then gave money to the neighboring farmers to pay off their mortgages.

Jesse James probably regarded himself as an idealist at heart, just as Dutch Schultz, "Two Gun" Crowley, Al Capone, and many other organized crime "godfathers" did generations later. The fact is that all people you meet have a high regard for themselves and like to be fine and unselfish in their own estimation.

J. Pierpont Morgan observed, in one of his analytical interludes, that a person usually has two good reasons for doing a thing: one that sounds good and a real one.

The person himself will think of the real reason. You don't need to emphasize that. But all of us, being idealists at heart, like to think of motives that sound good. So, in order to change people, appeal to the nobler motives.

Is that too idealistic to work in business? Let's see.

Let's take the case of Hamilton J. Farrell of the Farrell-Mitchell Company of Glenolden, Pennsylvania. Mr. Farrell had a disgruntled tenant who threatened to move. The tenant's lease still had four months to run; nevertheless, he served notice that he was vacating immediately, regardless of lease.

"These people had lived in my house all winter—the most expensive part of the year," Mr. Farrell said as he told the story to the class, "and I knew it would be difficult to rent the apartment again before fall. I could see all that rent income going over the hill and believe me, I saw red.

"Now, ordinarily, I would have waded into that tenant and advised him to read his lease again. I would have pointed out that if he moved, the full balance of his rent would fall due at once—and that I could, *and would*, take steps to collect.

"However, instead of flying off the handle and making a scene, I decided to try other tactics. So I started like this: 'Mr. Doe,' I said, 'I have listened to your story, and I still don't believe you intend to move. Years in the renting business have taught me something about human nature, and I sized you up in the first place as being a man of your word. In fact, I'm so sure of it that I'm willing to take a gamble.

" 'Now, here's my proposition. Lay your decision on the table for a few days and think it over. If you come back to me between now and the first of the month, when the rent is due, and tell me you still intend to move, I give you my word I will accept your decision as final. I will give you the privilege of moving and admit to myself I've been wrong in my judgment. But I still believe you're a man of your word and will live up to your contract. For after all, we are either man or monkeys—and the choice usually lies with ourselves!'

"Well, when the new month came around, this gentleman came to see me and paid his rent in person. He and his wife had talked it over, he said—and decided to stay. They had concluded that the only honorable thing to do was to live up to their lease."

When the late Lord Northcliffe found a newspaper using a picture of him which he didn't want published, he wrote the editor a letter. But did he say, "Please do not publish that picture of me anymore; *I* don't like it"? No, he appealed to a nobler motive. He appealed to the respect and love that all of us have for motherhood. He wrote, "Please do not publish that picture of me anymore. My mother doesn't like it."

When John D. Rockefeller, Jr., wished to stop newspaper photographers from snapping pictures of his children, he, too, appealed to the nobler motives. He didn't say: "I don't want the pictures published." No, he applead to the desire, deep in all of us, to refrain from harming children. He said: "You know how it is, boys. You've got children yourselves, some of you. And you know it's not good for youngsters to get too much publicity."

When Cyrus H. K. Curtis, a poor boy from Maine, was starting on the meteoric career which was destined to make him millions as owner of *The Saturday Evening Post* and the *Ladies Home Journal*, he couldn't afford to pay his contributors the prices that other magazines paid. He couldn't afford to hire first-class authors to write for money alone. So he appealed to their nobler motives. For example, he persuaded even Louisa May Alcott, the immortal author of *Little Women*, to write for him when she was at the flood tide of her fame; and he did it by offering to send a check for a hundred dollars, not to her, but to her favorite charity.

Right here the skeptic may say: "Oh, that stuff is all right for Northcliffe and Rockefeller or a sentimental novelist. But I'd like to see you make it work with the tough babies I have to collect bills from!"

You may be right. Nothing will work in all cases—and

nothing will work with all people. If you are satisfied with the results you are getting, why change? If you are not satisfied, why not experiment?

At any rate, I think you will enjoy reading this true story told by James L. Thomas, a former student of mine:

Six customers of a certain automobile company refused to pay their bills for servicing. None of the customers protested the entire bill, but each claimed that some one charge was wrong. In each case, the customer had signed for the work done, so the company knew it was right—and said so. That was the first mistake.

Here are the steps the credit department took to collect these overdue bills. Do you suppose they succeeded?

They called on the customers and told them bluntly that they had come to collect a bill that was long past due.

They made it very plain that the company was absolutely and unconditionally right; therefore, the customer was absolutely and unconditionally wrong.

They intimated that they, the company, knew more about automobiles than the customer could ever hope to know. So what was the argument about?

Result: They argued.

Did any of these methods reconcile the customer and settle the account? You can answer that one yourself.

At this stage of affairs, the credit manager was about to open fire with a battery of legal talent, when fortunately the matter came to the attention of the general manager. The manager investigated these defaulting clients and discovered that they all had the reputation of paying their bills promptly. Something was wrong here—something was drastically wrong about the method of collection. So he called in James L. Thomas and told him to collect these "uncollectible" accounts.

Here, in his words, are the steps Mr. Thomas took:

"My visit to each customer was likewise to collect a bill long past due—a bill that we knew was absolutely right. But I didn't say a word about that. I explained I had called to find out what it was the company had done, or failed to do.

"I made it clear that, until I heard the customer's story, I had no opinion to offer. I told him the company made no claims to being infallible.

"I told him I was interested only in his car, and that he knew more about his car than anyone else in the world; that he was the authority on the subject.

"I let him talk, and I listened to him with all the interest and sympathy that he wanted—and expected.

"Finally, when the customer was in a reasonable mood, I put the whole thing up to his sense of fair play. I appealed to the nobler motives. "First," I said, "I want you to know I also feel this matter has been badly mishandled. You've been inconvenienced and annoyed and irritated by one of our representatives. That should never have happened. I'm sorry and, as a representative of the company, I apologize. As I sat here and listened to your side of the story, I could not help being impressed by your fairness and patience. And now, because you are fair-minded and patient, I am going to ask you do to something for me. It's something that you can do better than anyone else, something you know more about than anyone else. Here is your bill; I know it is safe for me to adjust it, just as you would do if you were the president of my company. I am going to leave it all up to you. Whatever you say goes."

"Did he adjust the bill? He certainly did, and got quite a kick out of it. The bills ranged from $150 to $400—but did the customer give himself the best of it? Yes, one of them did! One of them refused to pay a penny of the disputed charge; but the other five all gave the company the best of it! And here's the cream of the whole thing: we delivered new cars to all six of these customers within the next two years!"

"Experience has taught me," says Mr. Thomas, "that when no information can be secured about the customer, the only sound basis on which to proceed is to assume that he or she is sincere, honest, truthful, and willing and anxious to pay the charges, once convinced they are correct. To put it differently and perhaps more clearly, people are honest and want to discharge their obligations. The exceptions to that rule are comparatively few, and I am convinced that the individuals who are inclined to chisel will in most cases react favorably if you make them feel that you consider them honest, upright, and fair."

Appeal to the nobler motives.

PART FOUR

WAYS TO CHANGE PEOPLE WITHOUT GIVING OFFENSE OR AROUSING RESENTMENT

If we intend to "Change People Without Giving Offense or Arousing Resentment," we must begin with an attitude of respect for, and acceptance of, the *person*. His response depends on our attitude.

18

How to Criticize—and Not Be Hated for It

Charles Schwab was passing through one of his steel mills one day at noon when he came across some of his employees smoking. Immediately above their heads was a sign that said "No Smoking." Did Schwab point to the sign and say, "Can't you read?" Oh, no, not Schwab. He walked over to the men, handed each one a cigar, and said, "I'll appreciate it, boys, if you will smoke these on the outside." They knew that he knew that they had broken a rule—and they admired him because he said nothing about it and gave them a little present and made them feel important. Couldn't keep from loving a man like that, could you?

John Wanamaker used the same technique. Wanamaker used to make a tour of his great store in Philadelphia every day. Once he saw a customer waiting at a counter. No one was paying the slightest attention to her. The salespeople? Oh, they were in a huddle at the far end of the counter laughing and talking among themselves. Wanamaker didn't say a word. Quietly slipping behind the counter, he waited on the woman himself and then handed the purchase to the salespeople to be wrapped as he went on his way.

Public officials are often criticized for not being accessible to their constituents. They are busy people, and the fault sometimes lies in overprotective assistants who don't want to overburden their bosses with too many visitors. Carl Langford, who had been mayor of Orlando, Florida, the home of Disney World, for many years, frequently admonished his staff to allow people to see him. He claimed he had an "open-door" policy; yet the citizens of his community were blocked by secretaries and administrators when they called.

Finally the mayor found the solution. He removed the door from his office! His aides got the message, and the mayor had a truly open administration from the day his door was symbolically thrown away.

Simply changing one three-letter word can often spell the difference between failure and success in changing people without giving offense or arousing resentment.

Many people begin their criticism with sincere praise followed by the word "but" and ending with a critical statement. For example, in trying to change a child's careless attitude toward studies, we might say, "We're really proud of you, Johnnie, for raising your grades this term. *But* if you had worked harder on your algebra, the results would have been better."

In this case, Johnnie might feel encouraged until he heard the word "but." He might then question the sincerity of the original praise. To him, the praise might seem only to be a contrived lead-in to a critical inference of failure. Credibility would be strained, and we probably would not achieve our objective of changing Johnnie's attitude toward his studies.

This could be easily overcome by changing the word "but" to "and." "We're really proud of you, Johnnie, for raising your grades this term, *and* if you continue the same conscientious efforts next term, your algebra grade can be up with all the others."

Now, Johnnie would accept the praise because there was no follow-up of an inference of failure. We have called his attention to the behavior we wished to change indirectly, and the chances are he will try to live up to our expectations.

Calling attention indirectly to someone's mistakes works wonders with sensitive people who may resent bitterly any direct criticism. Marge Jacob of Woonsocket, Rhode Island, told one of our classes how she convinced some sloppy construction workers to clean up after themselves when they were building additions to her house.

For the first few days of the work, when Mrs. Jacob returned from her job, she noticed that the yard was strewn with the cut ends of lumber. She didn't want to antagonize the builders, because they did excellent work. So after the workers had gone home, she and her children picked up and neatly piled all the lumber debris in a corner. The following morning she called the foreman to one side and said, "I'm really pleased with the way the front lawn was left last night; it is nice and clean and does not offend the neighbors." From that day forward the workers picked up and piled the debris to one side, and the foreman came in each day seeking approval of the condition the lawn was left in after a day's work.

One of the major areas of controversy between members of the army reserves and their regular army trainers is haircuts. The reservists consider themselves civilians (which they are most of the time) and resent having to cut their hair short.

Master Sergeant Harley Kaiser of the 542nd USAR School addressed himself to this problem when he was working with a group of reserve noncommissioned officers. As an old-time regular-army master sergeant, he might have been expected to yell at his troops and threaten them. Instead he chose to make his point indirectly.

"Gentlemen," he started, "you are leaders. You will be most effective when you lead by example. You must be the example for your men to follow. You know what the army

186 • How to Enjoy Your Life and Your Job

regulations say about haircuts. I am going to get my hair cut today, although it is still much shorter than some of yours. You look at yourself in the mirror, and if you feel you need a haircut to be a good example, we'll arrange time for you to visit the post barbershop."

The result was predictable. Several of the candidates did look in the mirror and went to the barbershop that afternoon and received "regulation" haircuts. Sergeant Kaiser commented the next morning that he already could see the development of leadership qualities in some of the members of the squad.

On March 8, 1887, the eloquent Henry Ward Beecher died. The following Sunday, Lyman Abbott was invited to speak in the pulpit left silent by Beecher's passing. Eager to do his best, he wrote, rewrote, and polished his sermon with the meticulous care of a Flaubert. Then he read it to his wife. It was poor—as most written speeches are. She might have said, if she had had less judgment, "Lyman, that is terrible. That'll never do. You'll put people to sleep. It reads like an encyclopedia. You ought to know better than that after all the years you have been preaching. For heaven's sake, why don't you talk like a human being? Why don't you act natural? You'll disgrace yourself if you ever read that stuff."

That's what she *might* have said. And, if she had, you know what would have happened. And she knew too. So, she merely remarked that it would make a excellent article for the *North American Review*. In other words, she praised it and at the same time subtly suggested that it wouldn't do as a speech. Lyman Abbott saw the point, tore up his carefully prepared manuscript, and preached without even using notes.

An effective way to correct others' mistakes is to . . .

Call attention to people's mistakes indirectly.

19

Talk About Your Own Mistakes First

My niece, Josephine Carnegie, had come to New York to be my secretary. She was nineteen, had graduated from high school three years previously, and her business experience was a trifle more than zero. She became one of the most proficient secretaries west of Suez, but in the beginning, she was—well, susceptible to improvement. One day when I started to criticize her, I said to myself: "Just a minute, Dale Carnegie; just a minute. You are twice as old as Josephine. You have ten thousand times as much business experience. How can you possibly expect her to have your viewpoint, your judgment, your initiative—mediocre though they may be? And just a minute, Dale, what were you doing at nineteen? Remember the asinine mistakes and blunders you made? Remember the time you did this . . . and that . . . ?"

After thinking the matter over, honestly and impartially, I concluded that Josephine's batting average at nineteen was better than mine had been—and that, I'm sorry to confess, isn't paying Josephine much of a compliment.

So after that, when I wanted to call Josephine's attention to a mistake, I used to begin by saying, "You have made a mistake, Josephine, but the Lord knows, it's no worse than many I have made. You were not born with judgment. That comes only with experience, and you are better than I was at your age. I have been guilty of so many stupid, silly things myself, I have very little inclination to criticize you or anyone. But don't you think it would have been wiser if you had done so and so?"

It isn't nearly so difficult to listen to a recital of your faults if the person criticizing begins by humbly admitting that he, too, is far from impeccable.

E. G. Dillistone, an engineer in Brandon, Manitoba, Canada, was having problems with his new secretary. Letters he dictated were coming to his desk for signature with two or three spelling mistakes per page. Mr. Dillistone reported how he handled this:

"Like many engineers, I have not been noted for my excellent English or spelling. For years I have kept a little black thumb-index book for words I had trouble spelling. When it became apparent that merely pointing out the errors was not going to cause my secretary to do more proofreading and dictionary work, I resolved to take another approach. When the next letter came to my attention that had errors in it, I sat down with the typist and said:

" 'Somehow this word doesn't look right. It's one of the words I always have had trouble with. That's the reason I started this spelling book of mine. (I opened the book to the appropriate page.) Yes, here it is. I'm very conscious of the spelling now because people do judge us by our letters, and misspellings make us look less professional.'

"I don't know whether she copied my system or not, but since that conversation, her frequency of spelling errors has been significantly reduced."

The polished Prince Bernhard von Bülow learned the sharp necessity of doing this back in 1909. Von Bülow was then the imperial chancellor of Germany, and on the throne sat Wilhelm II—Wilhelm, the haughty; Wilhelm, the arrogant; Wilhelm, the last of the German kaisers, building an army and navy that he boasted could whip their weight in wildcats.

Then an astonishing thing happened. The kaiser said things, incredible things, things that rocked the continent and started a series of explosions heard around the world. To make matters worse, the kaiser made silly, egotistical, absurd announcements in public. He made them while he was a guest in England, and he gave his royal permission to have them printed in the *Daily Telegraph*. For example, he declared that he was the only German who felt friendly toward the English; that he was constructing a navy against the menace of Japan; that he, and he alone, had saved England from being humbled in the dust by Russia and France; that it had been *his* campaign plan that enabled England's Lord Roberts to defeat the Boers in South Africa; and so on and on.

No other such amazing words had ever fallen from the lips of a European king in peacetime within a hundred years. The entire continent buzzed with the fury of a hornet's nest. England was incensed. German statesmen were aghast. And in the midst of all this consternation, the kaiser became panicky and suggested to Prince von Bülow, the imperial chancellor, that he take the blame. Yes, he wanted von Bülow to announce that it was all his responsibility, that he had advised his monarch to say these incredible things.

"But Your Majesty," von Bülow protested, "it seems to me utterly impossible that anybody either in Germany or England could suppose me capable of having advised Your Majesty to say any such thing."

The moment those words were out of von Bülow's mouth, he realized he had made a grave mistake. The kaiser blew up.

"You consider me a donkey," he shouted, "capable of blunders you yourself could never have committed."

Von Bülow knew that he ought to have praised before he condemned; but since it was too late, he did the next best thing. He praised after he had criticized. And it worked a miracle.

"I'm far from suggesting that," he answered respectfully. "Your Majesty surpasses me in many respects; not only, of course, in naval and military knowledge, but above all, in natural science. I have often listened in admiration when Your Majesty explained the barometer, or wireless telegraphy, or the Roentgen rays. I am shamefully ignorant of all branches of natural science, have no notion of chemistry or physics, and am quite incapable of explaining the simplest of natural phenomena. But," von Bülow continued, "in compensation, I possess some historical knowledge and perhaps certain qualities useful in politics, especially in diplomacy."

The kaiser beamed. Von Bülow had praised him. Von Bülow had exalted him and humbled himself. The kaiser could forgive anything after that. "Haven't I always told you," he exclaimed with enthusiasm, "that we complete one another famously? We should stick together, and we will!"

He shook hands with von Bülow, not once, but several times. And later in the day he waxed so enthusiastic that he exclaimed with doubled fists, "If anyone says anything to me against Prince von Bülow, *I shall punch him in the nose.*"

Von Bülow saved himself in time—but, canny diplomat that he was, he nevertheless had made one error: he should have *begun* by talking about his own shortcomings and Wilhelm's superiority—not by intimating that the kaiser was a half-wit in need of a guardian.

If a few sentences humbling oneself and praising the

other party can turn a haughty, insulted kaiser into a staunch friend, imagine what humility and praise can do for you and me in our daily contacts. Rightly used, they will work veritable miracles in human relations.

Admitting one's own mistakes—even when one hasn't corrected them—can help convince somebody to change his or her behavior. This was illustrated more recently by Clarence Zerhusen of Timonium, Maryland, when he discovered his fifteen-year-old son was experimenting with cigarettes.

"Naturally, I didn't want David to smoke," Mr. Zerhusen told us, "but his mother and I smoked cigarettes; we were giving him a bad example all the time. I explained to Dave how I started smoking at about his age and how the nicotine had gotten the best of me and now it was nearly impossible for me to stop. I reminded him how irritating my cough was and how he had been after me to give up cigarettes not many years before.

"I didn't exhort him to stop or make threats or warn him about their dangers. All I did was point out how I was hooked on cigarettes and what it had meant to me.

"He thought about it for a while and decided he wouldn't smoke until he had graduated from high school. As the years went by David never did start smoking and has no intention of ever doing so.

"As a result of that conversation I made the decision to stop smoking myself, and with the support of my family, I have succeeded."

A good leader follows this principle:

Talk about your own mistakes before criticizing the other person.

20

No One Likes to Take Orders

I once had the pleasure of dining with Mrs. Ida Tarbell, the dean of American biographers. When I told her I was writing this book, we began discussing this all-important subject of getting along with people, and she told me that while she was writing her biography of Owen D. Young, she interviewed a man who had sat for three years in the same office with Mr. Young. This man declared that during all that time he had never heard Owen D. Young give a direct order to anyone. He always gave suggestions, not orders. Owen D. Young never said, for example, "Do this or do that," or "Don't do this or don't do that." He would say, "You might consider this," or "Do you think that would work?" Frequently he would say, after he had dictated a letter, "What do you think of this?" In looking over a letter of one of his assistants, he would say, "Maybe if we were to phrase it this way it would be better." He always gave people the opportunity to do things themselves; he never told his assistants to do things; he let them do them, let them learn from their mistakes.

A technique like that makes it easy for a person to

correct errors. A technique like that saves a person's pride and gives him or her a feeling of importance. It encourages cooperation instead of rebellion.

Resentment caused by a brash order may last a long time—even if the order was given to correct an obviously bad situation. Dan Santarelli, a teacher at a vocational school in Wyoming, Pennsylvania, told one of our classes how one of his students had blocked the entraceway to one of the school's shops by illegally parking his car in it. One of the other instructors stormed into the classroom and asked in an arrogant tone, "Whose car is blocking the driveway?" When the student who owned the car responded, the instructor screamed: "Move that car and move it right now, or I'll wrap a chain around it and drag it out of there."

Now that student was wrong. The car should not have been parked there. But from that day on, not only did that student resent the instructor's action, but all the students in the class did everything they could to give the instructor a hard time and make his job unpleasant.

How could he have handled it differently? If he had asked in a friendly way, "Whose car is in the driveway?" and then suggested that if it were moved, other cars could get in and out, the student would have gladly moved it and neither he nor his classmates would have been upset and resentful.

Asking questions not only makes an order more palatable; it often stimulates the creativity of the persons whom you ask. People are more likely to accept an order if they have had a part in the decision that caused the order to be issued.

When Ian Macdonald of Johannesburg, South Africa, the general manager of a small manufacturing plant specializing in precision machine parts, had the opportunity to accept a very large order, he was convinced that he would not meet the promised delivery date. The work already scheduled in the shop and the short completion time needed for this order made it seem impossible for him to accept the order.

Instead of pushing his people to accelerate their work and rush the order through, he called everybody together, explained the situation to them, and told them how much it would mean to the company and to them if they could make it possible to produce the order on time. Then he started asking questions:

"Is there anything we can do to handle this order?"

"Can anyone think of different ways to process it through the shop that will make it possible to take the order?"

"Is there any way to adjust our hours or personnel assignments that would help?"

The employees came up with many ideas and insisted that he take the order. They approached it with a "We can do it" attitude, and the order was accepted, produced, and delivered on time.

An effective leader will . . .

Ask questions instead of giving direct orders.

21

Let the Other Person Save Face

Years ago the General Electric Company was faced with the delicate task of removing Charles Steinmetz from the head of a department. Steinmetz, a genius of the first magnitude when it came to electricity, was a failure as the head of the calculating department. Yet the company didn't dare offend the man. He was indispensable—and highly sensitive. So they gave him a new title. They made him consulting engineer of the General Electric Company—a new title for work he was already doing—and let someone else head the department.

Steinmetz was happy.

So were the officers of G.E. They had gently maneuvered their most temperamental star, and they had done it without a storm—by letting him save face.

Letting someone save face! How important, how vitally important, that is! And how few of us ever stop to think of it! We ride roughshod over the feelings of others, getting our own way, finding fault, issuing threats, criticizing a child or an employee in front of others, without even considering the hurt to the other person's pride. Whereas a few minutes' thought, a considerate word or two, a genuine understanding of the other person's attitude, would go so far toward alleviating the sting!

Let's remember this the next time we are faced with the distasteful necessity of discharging or reprimanding an employee.

"Firing employees is not much fun. Getting fired is even less fun." (I'm quoting now from a letter written me by Marshall A. Granger, a certified public accountant.) "Our business is mostly seasonal. Therefore we have to let a lot of people go when the income tax rush is over.

"It's a byword in our profession that no one enjoys wielding the ax. Consequently, the custom has developed of getting it over as soon as possible, and usually in the following way: 'Sit down, Mr. Smith. The season's over, and we don't seem to see any more assignments for you. Of course, you understand you were employed only for the busy season anyhow, etc., etc.'

"The effect on these people is one of disappointment and a feeling of being 'let down.' Most of them are in the accounting field for life, and they retain no particular love for the firm that drops them so casually.

"I recently decided to let our seasonal personnel go with a little more tact and consideration. So I call each one in only after carefully thinking over his or her work during the winter. And I've said something like this: 'Mr. Smith, you've done a fine job (if he has). That time we sent you to Newark, you had a tough assignment. You were on the spot, but you came through with flying colors, and we want you to know the firm is proud of you. You've got the stuff— you're going a long way, wherever you're working. This firm believes in you, and is rooting for you, and we don't want you to forget it.'

"Effect? The people go away feeling a lot better about being fired. They don't feel 'let down.' They know that if we had work for them, we'd keep them on. And when we need them again, they come to us with a keen personal affection."

At one session of our course, two class members discussed the negative effects of faultfinding versus the positive effects of letting the other person save face.

Fred Clark of Harrisburg, Pennsylvania, told of an incident that occurred in his company: "At one of our production meetings, a vice-president was asking very pointed questions of one of our production supervisors regarding a production process. His tone of voice was aggressive and aimed at pointing out faulty performance on the part of the supervisor. Not wanting to be embarrassed in front of his peers, the supervisor was evasive in his responses. This caused the vice-president to lose his temper, berate the supervisor, and accuse him of lying.

"Any working relationship that might have existed prior to this encounter was destroyed in a few brief moments. This supervisor, who was basically a good worker, was useless to our company from that time on. A few months later he left our firm and went to work for a competitor, where I understand he is doing a fine job."

Another class member, Anna Mazzone, related how a similar incident had occurred at her job—but what a difference in approach and results! Ms. Mazzone, a marketing specialist for a food packer, was given her first major assignment—the test marketing of a new product. She told the class: "When the results of the test came in, I was devastated. I had made a serious error in my planning, and the entire test had to be done all over again. To make this worse, I had no time to discuss it with my boss before the meeting in which I was to make my report on the project.

"When I was called on to give the report, I was shaking with fright. I had all I could do to keep from breaking down, but I resolved I would not cry and have all those men make

remarks about women not being able to handle an assignment because they are too emotional. I made my report
briefly and stated that due to an error I would repeat the
study before the next meeting. I sat down, expecting my
boss to blow up.

"Instead, he thanked me for my work and remarked
that it was not unusual for a person to make an error on a
new project and that he had confidence that the repeat
survey would be accurate and meaningful to the company.
He assured me, in front of my colleagues, that he had faith
in me and knew I had done my best, and that my lack of
experience, not my lack of ability, was the reason for the
failure.

"I left that meeting with my head up in the air and with
the determination that I would never let that boss of mine
down again."

Even if we are right and the other person is definitely
wrong, we only destroy ego by causing someone to lose
face. The legendary French aviation pioneer and author
Antoine de Saint-Exupéry wrote: "I have no right to say or
do anything that diminishes a man in his own eyes. What
matters is not what I think of him, but what he thinks of
himself. Hurting a man in his dignity is a crime."

A real leader will always . . .

Let the other person save face.

In a Nutshell

How to Stop Worrying and Start Living

1. Do not imitate others.
2. Apply these four good working habits:
   a. Clear your desk of all papers except those relating to the immediate problem at hand.
   b. Do things in the order of their importance.
   c. When you face a problem, solve it then and there if you have the facts necessary to make a decision.
   d. Learn to organize, deputize, and supervise.
3. Learn to relax at your work.
4. Put enthusiasm into your work.
5. Count your blessings—not your troubles.
6. Remember that unjust criticism is often a disguised compliment.
7. Do the very best you can.

RULES FROM
How to Win Friends and Influence People

1. Don't criticize, condemn, or complain.
2. Give honest, sincere appreciation.
3. Arouse in the other person an eager want.
4. Become genuinely interested in other people.

5. Make the other person feel important—and do it sincerely.
6. Show respect for the other person's opinions. Never say, "You're wrong."
7. Begin in a friendly way.
8. Get the other person saying "Yes, yes" immediately.
9. Let the other person feel that the idea is his or hers.
10. Appeal to the nobler motives.
11. Call attention to people's mistakes indirectly.
12. Talk about your own mistakes before criticizing the other person.
13. Ask questions instead of giving direct orders.
14. Let the other person save face.

Index

More Books from Vermilion

The prices below were correct at the time of going to press

❑ 07493 0791 9	**New Arthritis and Common Sense:** **A Complex Guide to Effective Relief**	Dale Alexander	£6.99
❑ 07493 0938 5	**The Courage to Heal**	Ellen Bass and Laura Davis	£10.99
❑ 07493 0856 7	**The Body Has Its Reason: Anti-exercise and Self-Awareness** Therese Bertherat and Carol Bernstein		£4.99
❑ 07493 0579 7	**How to Develop Self-Confidence and** **Influence People by Public Speaking**	Dale Carnegie	£7.99
❑ 07493 0593 2	**How to Enjoy Your Life and Your Job**	Dale Carnegie	£7.99
❑ 07493 0723 4	**How to Stop Worrying and Start Living**	Dale Carnegie	£7.99
❑ 07493 0784 6	**How to Win Friends and Influence People**	Dale Carnegie	£7.99
❑ 07493 0577 0	**The Quick and Easy Way to Effective Speaking**	Dale Carnegie	£7.99
❑ 07493 0246 1	**Overcoming Overeating**	Jane Hirschmann & Carol Munter	£6.99
❑ 07493 0713 7	**Living Together Feeling Alone**	Dr Dan Kiley	£6.99
❑ 07493 0933 4	**The Amazing Results of Positive Thinking**	Norman Vincent Peale	£7.99
❑ 07493 1341 2	**Courage and Confidence**	Norman Vincent Peale	£7.99
❑ 07493 0719 6	**Inspiring Messages for Daily Living**	Norman Vincent Peale	£7.99
❑ 07493 0858 3	**The Positive Way to Change Your Life**	Norman Vincent Peale	£7.99
❑ 07493 0821 4	**The Power of Positive Living**	Norman Vincent Peale	£7.99
❑ 07493 0715 3	**The Power of Positive Thinking**	Norman Vincent Peale	£7.99
❑ 07493 0567 3	**The Power of Positive Thinking for Young People** Norman Vincent Peale		£7.99
❑ 07493 0254 2	**Families and How to Survive Them**	Robin Skinner and John Cleese	£7.99
❑ 07493 2320 5	**Life and How to Survive It**	Robin Skinner and John Cleese	£7.99
❑ 07493 1041 3	**How to Survive in Spite of Your Parents**	Dr Margaret Reihnhold	£7.99
❑ 07493 1264 5	**Living with ME: A Self Help Guide**	Dr Charles Shepherd	£7.99
❑ 07493 1656 X	**Victims No Longer**	Mike Lew	£9.99
❑ 07493 2665 4	**The Handbook of Alternative and Complementary Medicine** Stephen Fulder		£12.99
❑ 07493 2289 6	**Your Child's Symptoms Explained**	Dr David Haslam	£7.99
❑ 07493 0936 9	**The Courage to Grieve**	Judith Tatelbaum	£6.99